D0445404

# Creativity and Divergent Thinking:
# A Task-Specific Approach

# Creativity and Divergent Thinking: A Task-Specific Approach

## John Baer

LAWRENCE ERLBAUM ASSOCIATES, PUBLISHERS

1993    Hillsdale, New Jersey                    Hove and London

Lawrence Erlbaum Associates, Inc., Publishers
365 Broadway
Hillsdale, New Jersey 07642

**Library of Congress Cataloging-in-Publication Data**

---

Baer, John.
        Creativity and divergent thinking: a task specific approach / John Baer.
            p. cm.
        Includes bibliographical references and index.
        ISBN 0-8058-1295-4
        1. Creative ability. 2. Divergent thinking. 3. Creative thinking. I. Title.
    BF408.B325 1993
    153.3'5—dc20                                                                    92-31470
                                                                                        CIP

---

Books published by Lawrence Erlbaum Associates are printed on acid-free paper, and their bindings
are chosen for strength and durability.

Printed in the United States of America
10  9  8  7  6  5  4  3  2  1

# Contents

# Preface

Unlike some topics in psychology, little explanation is needed for having an interest in creativity. Everyone has at one time or another marveled at the human ability to discover and invent new and interesting things and ideas—and, perhaps, at the equally human failure sometimes to rise above the quotidian. Most of us have also wished that we could be more creative, in our work and in our play. And all of us have on occasion proposed armchair theories and listened to others' ideas about what makes a person "creative," hoping thereby to gain some understanding of this most wonderful mystery.

This book is about the last question, what it takes to be "creative." As the quotation marks suggest, I have trouble using the word without making some caveat; as will be explained in the book, my research has suggested that there is a problem with stating the question this way, in such general terms. But the nature of creativity—more specifically, the nature of creative thinking, and how a general theory such as divergent thinking can help us understand creative performance in a variety of contexts—is nonetheless what this book is about.

## ACKNOWLEDGMENTS

This book grew out of research conducted at Rutgers, the State University of New Jersey. The research reported in chapters 4 and 5 was supported under a National Science Foundation Graduate Fellowship, a Rutgers Graduate Scholars Award, and a Rutgers Excellence Fellowship; some of this research was previously reported in the *Creativity Research Journal* (Baer, 1991, pp. 23–40) and in the Berlyne Prize address at the annual meeting of the American Psychological Association (Baer, 1992). Preparation of this volume was supported, in part, by a grant from the Educational Testing Service. I thank the NSF, Rutgers, the *Creativity Research Journal*, the Berlyne Prize committee, and the ETS for their support that, in a variety of ways, made this book possible.

The people who helped me develop the ideas reported in this volume, and who helped shape the research that tested those ideas, predate my work as a psychologist. A partial list would include, first, my parents, Janice Baer and John Baer (Sr.), who taught me in different ways the importance of creativity, and who have encouraged my efforts to understand it; Sarita and Fred Kuhner, who have always been supportive of my work; many friends, students, and colleagues who have stimulated ideas and discussions over the years; Mark Runco, the editor of

*Creativity Research Journal,* without whose encouragement these ideas would probably not have been brought together in book form; Erich Labouvie, whose statistical help was invaluable; and Judith Hudson, who helped shape much of the research reported in chapters 4 and 5 through her questions and comments. Although whatever mistakes and wrong directions the reader may discover in the text are my responsibility alone, these people share credit for whatever merit there is in this book, and I wish to thank them for the different kinds of guidance they have each provided me.

My daughter Heather, who is currently 14 years old and one of the most all-around creative people I know, has been an inspiration of another sort—and also a willing co-investigator, who gamely tried out and helped shape many of the tasks I was later to use in my research studies.

Finally, and most importantly, I must thank the poet and teacher Sylvia Baer (who happens to be my spouse), whose creativity remains a mystery to me but whose ideas, gentle criticisms, and patience have been with me every step of the way in conducting the research, developing the ideas, and finding the words that make up this book.

*John Baer*

# 1

# Introduction

## CONTEXT AND GOALS

A central controversial issue in creativity research and theory is whether creativity is (a) a general capacity that influences an individual's performance across many domains, or (b) a widely diverse collection of skills and knowledge, each contributing to creative performance in only a single domain (Bamberger, 1990). The former assumption—that general creativity-relevant traits, skills, attitudes, or habits of thought exist—has guided much research and theory in creativity (see, e.g., Amabile, 1983; Darley, Glucksberg, & Kinchla, 1986; Kogan, 1983; Perkins, 1981; Tardif & Sternberg, 1988; Torrance & Presbury, 1984). This monolithic view has recently been challenged, however, by a number of writers (see, e.g., Gardner, 1988; Gruber & Davis, 1988; Runco, 1987; Tardif & Sternberg, 1988; Winner, 1982).

There are many reasons for hoping that a general theory of creativity can be constructed to (a) explain creative thought processes, (b) predict creative behavior, and (c) demonstrate an underlying unity among diverse creative activities and productions. From a theoretical point of view, a general theory would be both more efficient and more elegant; and from a practical perspective, a one-size-fits-all theory would make the testing and training of creativity-relevant skills easier and more effective.

Psychologists working in fields other than creativity have also, for similar reasons, been attracted to general theories that can account for wide-ranging observations and connect seemingly disparate phenomena. Consider, for example, the hard-to-eradicate appeal of IQ scores (e.g., Jensen, 1980; Snow & Lohman, 1984), which lingers despite both (a) arguments dating back to the originator of IQ testing, Alfred Binet, stating that "intelligence is not a simple indivisible function" (Binet, 1911/1962, p. 150); and (b) nearly a century of accumulated psychometric evidence that single-factor theories cannot adequately represent human cognition (Gardner, 1983; Sternberg, 1988). Similarly, there has been an almost century-long struggle in educational psychology between those who have argued for and against the long-cherished belief that the study of certain subjects (such as Latin) will train

1

the mind to learn more readily any subject one chooses to study. As early as 1903, Thorndike presented correlational evidence that "the mind is a host of highly particularized and independent abilities" (Thorndike, 1903, p. 39) and that success in one field of study was at most mildly predictive of success in other fields. Despite general consensus among educational psychologists that Thorndike was right, the appeal of theories that emphasize general, easily transferable cognitive skills or traits remains with us because of the power to improve thinking and learning that such skills or traits could provide (Costa, 1985; Gardner, 1983; Kaplan, 1990; Mayer, 1983, 1987; Smith, Sera, & Gattuso, 1988; Sternberg & Davidson, 1986; Wiggins, 1989).

The appeal of theories positing teachable skills that improve overall intellectual competence is also evidenced in advertising claims for a wide variety of training programs. *Wff 'N Proof,* a game of symbolic logic, claims in its advertisements an average increase of 20 IQ-test points after just 3 weeks of playing the game. Edward de Bono's (1985) CoRT program claims that "so basic is thinking as a skill that the same CoRT lessons have been used by children in the jungles of South America and by top executives of the Ford Motor Company" (p. 208). And on a recent National Public Radio broadcast, a dance instructor who was being interviewed averred that learning tap dancing "trains the mind" and makes all other kinds of learning easier. These claims are similar to the belief that learning Latin can improve thinking of all kinds and in all subjects—a claim that is only now being generally abandoned, almost a century after Thorndike's (1903) initial attempts to dispel it (Mayer, 1987).

The search for general, all-encompassing theories has by no means been limited to psychology (or advertising). A primary goal of physics is to find "a complete, consistent, unified theory that would include ... all partial theories as approxima-tions" (Hawking, 1988, p. 155). Einstein spent most of his later years searching for such a unified theory, and although he was unsuccessful, the search for a grand unified theory, or "Theory of Everything," has captured the imagination of many of the world's foremost scientists (Davies, 1984; Riordan & Schramm, 1991).

Despite their popularity, however, general, context-free theories have been on the defensive in recent years in many fields. Feminist scholarship has challenged the hegemony of such models in the physical, natural, and social sciences (Belenky, Clinchy, Goldberger, & Tarule, 1986; Fausto-Sterling, 1991; Harding, 1986; Gilligan, 1982; Gilligan & Attanucci, 1988; Nelson, 1990). Challenges to the universal nature of theories have been especially common in the various sub-disciplines that make up psychology. For example, in developmental psychology, the effects of domain-specific knowledge on stages of cognitive development are widely acknowledged (Chi, 1978; DeLisi & Staudt, 1980; Fivush & Hudson, 1990; Flavell, 1985); in both cognitive psychology and behavioral neuroscience, con-nectionist/neural network models challenge what might now be thought of as "classical" information-processing models (for a range of perspectives on how connectionist models differ from the information-processing approach, see Berei-ter, 1991; Edelman, 1987, 1989; McClelland, Rumelhart, & the PDP Research Group, 1986; Pinker & Prince, 1987; Rumelhart, McClelland, & the PDP Research

Group, 1986; Smolensky, 1988); and in social, educational, and clinical psychology, new epistemologies—new world views that are more contextualist in nature—have become increasingly popular (Cantor & Kihlstrom, 1987; Kramer & Bopp, 1989; McKerrow & McKerrow, 1991; Pintrich, 1990).

This brief overview of the question of the level of universality at which it is most appropriate to pitch scientific theories—that is, whether science is better served by general, context-transcending theories or particularistic, context-specific theories—demonstrates that this debate extends beyond both creativity research and the field of psychology. But what can this context tells us about how to proceed with research and theory-building in creativity?

One answer to this question is a simple acknowledgment of the importance, and the complexity, of the issue. From this perspective, many fields of science can be seen to be wrestling with essentially the same difficult question. Although recognizing that creativity theory is not alone in struggling with the generality–specificity issue offers little guidance in the search for solutions to this question in creativity theory and research, it does promote an appreciation of the general significance of the issue.

A second answer also relates to this sharing of a common theme by suggesting that, through an analysis of the debates, evidence, and (where they exist) conclusions being produced elsewhere in psychology and in the other sciences, creativity theorists may be able learn lessons that will enable them to solve creativity's own unique versions of the generality–specificity issue more efficiently and more thoroughly. There is, of course, some irony in taking what might be termed a *universal* perspective on these issues. Because these issues in the various sciences all seek to determine how much to focus on the particular (be it a particular context, a particular task or domain, or a particular subgroup or subset that illustrates the failure of general rules or theories), one may argue that simply taking such a perspective is in itself an endorsement of the universal approach and a denial of the validity of the particularistic model.

A third answer to the question, "What can the particularist–universalist debates in the various sciences teach creativity theory?" comes from examining the success of these two approaches in fields more (and less) like creativity theory. There is, perhaps, a rough continuum in science, with physics near one end and the social sciences nearer the other. *Hard* and *soft* are the terms most often applied to the ends of this continuum, although *contextually stripped* and *contextually rich* (Fausto-Sterling, 1991, p. 11; see also Harding, 1986, for the origin and a fuller development of this approach to analyzing the scientific hierarchy) are alternative terms to describe the endpoints of the same continuum. Universal theories have been successful, and continue to hold sway, in physics, which is generally considered the *hardest* (and most contextually stripped) of the sciences. Most of the other sciences, including the social sciences, have attempted to capitalize on physics' success by imitating physics' preference for producing grand, unified theories, a hierarchical view of the sciences that Fausto-Sterling (1991) dubbed "physics envy" (p. 10). But particularistic challenges to universal theories have been most successful in the *softer,* contextually rich sciences, and there is currently much "debate ... whether physics (at least, classical physics) can serve as a model for biology and other sciences" (Nelson, 1990, p. 219).

Without entering directly into this debate about the appropriateness of modelling other sciences (like psychology) on physics, it is nonetheless possible to see that creativity theory (and, arguably, all of psychology) currently stands closer to the soft, contextually rich end of the soft/hard, contextually rich/contextually stripped continuum. This allows us to recognize that particularistic claims are likely, at least at this stage in their development, to be relevant to creativity theory. This does not mean that we should abandon larger, more general theories, because even if we accept that more narrow, particularistic theories are inevitable, this acceptance does not tell us along which lines we should subdivide the concept, topic, or field of creativity. Do we need different models for creativity based on age, culture, or gender? On educational background? On the domain, or the specific task, being undertaken? Perhaps there are many such lines to be drawn, but they must be drawn on the basis on research, not a priori theorizing. It is one of the goals of this book to demonstrate one such set of lines that should be drawn—a set of lines that describes a universe of task-specific constraints —and to propose how creativity theory will be enriched by adopting the particularistic approach defined by this set of task-specific considerations.

Accepting the need to draw lines that subdivide creativity theory does not preclude the possibility that larger theories will, at some point, be more successful in explaining creativity than is currently possible. Nor does it mean that the larger theories we now have—in particular, divergent-thinking theories of creativity—are devoid of meaning. Much of what follows, although critical of general theories of creativity (and especially of divergent-thinking theories), grows directly out of such large, universal approaches. It is therefore a goal of this book not only to show where such general approaches fail us, but also to demonstrate in what ways they can still guide both our thinking about creativity theory and our efforts to improve creative performance through instruction.

It is, finally, a goal of this book to show how at least a part of the work of two large groups of creativity researchers—those who take a particularistic stance, and those who espouse more universal theories—can be brought together into a single research paradigm.

## AN OVERVIEW OF THE BOOK

The term *creativity* has a wide range of meanings, many, but not all, of which are the subject of this book. One recent meta-theoretical analysis of creativity (Johnson-Laird, 1988b) argued, from an information-processing viewpoint, for three kinds of creativity, which I label *real time, multi-stage,* and *paradigm-shifting* creativity.

*Real-Time Creativity.* (Also called "on-line" in computer jargon.) This refers to creative performance within some genre under time constraints that make performance basically spontaneous, with no opportunity for revision—as in jazz, modern dance, or other forms of improvisation; in everyday conversation; or in any kind of extemporaneous performance or problem-solving task (such as reacting to emergency situations). Because performance of this kind does not allow sufficient time for the generation of a wide range of alternative solutions followed by a thoughtful selection among those candidate solutions, creative performance in real time requires tight constraints on the kinds of possible solutions that will be generated. Choice among candidate solutions in this model is essentially arbitrary, in Johnson-Laird's (1988b) view, and therefore all the candidate solutions that are generated must meet the task constraints. This imposes significant limitations on the degree of variability that can be tolerated among the candidate solutions. Johnson-Laird (1987) likened this real-time model of creativity to Lamarck's theory of evolution because the previous experience must guide the solution-generation process, rather than allowing an essentially random generation of ideas. This kind of real-time creative performance has received little attention in the creativity literature, making Johnson-Laird's attempts to model it using computer programs that create improvised jazz bass lines especially interesting. In the present analysis, however, real-time creativity is primarily of interest because it provides a contrasting model that helps to clarify the nature of the second, multistage model.

*Multistage Creativity.* This refers to creative performance within an established domain under conditions that allow sufficient time for evaluating and revising a variety of possible solutions. Creative performance of this type can be characterized as multistage because the generation of possible solutions follows a set of criteria that differs from the criteria by which optimal solutions are later judged. In the generation stage, the criteria for producing candidate solutions can be quite flexible, because unlike real-time creative performance, this multistage model can tolerate the generation of solutions that do not meet minimal task constraints. The two stages of this model (generation of ideas and selection of solutions) allow the process of multistage creativity to tolerate more diversity in its initial generation stage because there is an opportunity at the next stage to reject unworkable solutions. This multistage model thus allows a much wider range of possible solutions than the single-stage real-time model, in which the constraints on solution generation must be tight because there is no solution-evaluation stage prior to performance. It is, of course, possible (and, I believe, quite reasonable) to think of the distinction between real-time and multistage creative performances as a series of points along a continuum rather than as two discrete processes. The degree to which a performance is considered to allow multistage processing depends on the nature of whatever limitations are placed on the second, evaluative stage. These variations in the time available for evaluating competing candidate solutions in turn allow varying degrees of flexibility or "looseness" in the criteria used to guide the generation of candidate solutions.

*Paradigm-Shifting Creativity.* This refers to creative performances that result in fundamental changes in the nature of the domain in which the creator is working—such as changes in the way the domain itself is conceptualized, or changes in the options available to those who later work and solve problems in that domain. In this kind of creativity, Johnson-Laird argued (1988b), there can be no prior constraints on the kinds of candidate solutions that are generated. He therefore referred to this model as a "neo-Darwinian" process, and argued that "a neo-Darwinian procedure is the only mechanism available if there is no way in which the generative process can be guided by selective constraints" (p. 218). This is an extreme-case argument, however, because completely random idea generation would be a hopelessly time-consuming enterprise, and Johnson-Laird (1988b) himself acknowledged that "the productive use of knowledge is a central part of genius" (p. 218). It may prove, as Johnson-Laird suggested, far more difficult to discover the cognitive processes that support creativity of the highest order than to find the mechanisms that underlie real-time and multistage creativity; however, the fact that it may be more difficult to find, in Johnson-Laird's (1988b) words, "tractable computational algorithms for producing successful innovations" (p. 218) does not allow us to assume that the underlying processes are essentially different from those that underlie the quotidian, garden-variety creative performances that do not result in paradigm shifts. The distinction between paradigm-shifting and multistage creativity may, like the distinction between real-time and multistage creativity, be one of degree rather than a firm categorical difference. Although it will likely prove impossible to draw firm distinctions between different levels of creative performance, it may nonetheless be useful to analyze creative genius, on one hand, and the kinds of thinking that underlie everyday problem solving and garden-variety creativity, on the other, using different lenses, such as the meta-theoretical models that Johnson-Laird proposed.

Johnson-Laird's (1988b) analysis is a useful guide for specifying the kinds of creativity on which we are focusing attention. There are those creativity researchers and theorists, like Howard Gruber (1981; Gruber & Davis, 1988) and his many associates (many of whose works are collected in Wallace & Gruber, 1989), whose work focuses on the creativity of individuals whose genius is widely acknowledged. In fact, Gruber (Gruber & Davis, 1988) argued against "the use of inappropriate populations, such as ... unselected high school students. Although these are certainly valuable and interesting human beings, usually we can have no guarantee that the sample taken includes a single person who is functioning creatively" (p. 246). Under the definition of creativity that guides Gruber's work, much of the creativity that falls under both real-time and multistage creativity is simply not creativity, and therefore cannot tell us anything about the cognitive processes that underlie creative performance.

Among creativity theorists who argue for domain specificity, there is a tendency to focus on creativity of the highest order—the kind of creativity that leads to eminence in a field. And those who focus on creativity of the highest order tend, in turn, toward a domain-specific approach to the nature of creativity (Csikszentmihalyi, 1988, 1990; Gruber, 1981; Gruber & Davis, 1988; Tardif & Sternberg, 1988; Wallace & Gruber, 1989).

In contrast, those who view creativity as a more general trait tend to see creativity as a continuum, with genius at one end and everyday problem solving at the other. The distinction between multistage and paradigm-shifting creativity are considered matters of degree that do not reflect different underlying cognitive processes. Most of the divergent-thinking theories and measurement strategies (discussed in some detail in chapter 2) fall into this category. Because genius is hard to find, researchers in the "general trait" camp typically run studies that compare what might be termed the *garden-variety* creative performances of ordinary subjects under different experimentally controlled conditions.

In a series of studies (reported in part in Baer, 1991, 1992; but see chapters 4 and 5 in this volume for more complete details and for additional research results not reported elsewhere), I have adapted some of the techniques of the "continuum" school of creativity (especially those of Amabile, 1983) for use in testing the question of the generality of creative performance of ordinary subjects in various domains. My focus has been on the creative performance of unselected subjects working without significant time constraints (corresponding to multistage creativity). I asked subjects ranging in age from 7 to 40 years to produce poems, stories, collages, equations, and mathematical word problems. These products were all judged by groups of experts in their respective fields for creativity, and the results of these expert judgments consistently showed a high degree of interrater reliability.

As McShane (1991) noted, "domains may overlap, either by having similar representations (i.e., some mapping function exists between the representations) or similar procedures. When this occurs, it is reasonable to expect that skill in one domain will correlate with skill in another" (p. 318). One must assume, then, that if general-purpose, domain-transcending creative-thinking processes, distinct from those skills measured by standard aptitude or achievement tests, make substantial contributions to creative performance on different tasks, and if there are individual differences in how well subjects employ these thinking skills, then subjects who perform more creatively than their peers on one task should, other things being equal, tend to perform more creatively on other tasks in different domains. Similarly, low creativity on one task should be predictive of low creativity on other tasks.

The results of these studies (which are reviewed in chapter 4) have consistently favored a task-specific view of the skills underlying creative performance. Analyses of the expert ratings of the products made by subjects of all ages indicate that creative performance on one task is not predictive of creative performance on other tasks, including those that might normally be considered to fall into the same domain, such as the writing of poetry and the writing of stories. Creative performance on the tasks used in these studies has accurately predicted the level of creative performance on the same task at later testing dates, indicating a degree of stability in one's creativity on particular tasks, but the correlations with ratings for creativity on other tasks have been small and insignificant, hovering closely around zero. Scores on divergent-thinking tests have also not reliably predicted creative performance on any of the tasks. These results argue strongly against the existence of a general creative capacity (and against the importance of divergent thinking, a prime candidate for such a general creativity-relevant skill). They also argue against a domain-specific theory of creativity such as that proposed by Gardner (1983, 1988), because tasks in the same domain have followed the same pattern of noncorrelation as tasks in different domains. Creativity-relevant skills appear to be quite narrowly applicable, perhaps of use only on specific tasks.

The claim that general creative-thinking skills do not exist is a strong one, with wide implications. One set of implications centers around the divergent-production theory of creativity (Guilford, 1950, 1956, 1967; Guilford & Hoepfner, 1971), whose direct descendents, the various divergent-thinking theories of creativity, have dominated creativity theory and research (Crockenberg, 1972; Heausler & Thompson, 1988; Kagan, 1988; Kaplan, 1990; Kogan, 1983; Mayer, 1983; Mc-Crae, Arenberg, & Costa, 1987; Rose & Lin, 1984; Runco, 1986b; Runco & Albert, 1990; Torrance, 1972a, 1972b, 1984, 1990; Torrance & Presbury, 1984; Treffinger, 1986; Wallace, Goldstein, & Nathan, 1990; Wallach, 1970; Wallach & Kogan, 1965a, 1965b). Although Guilford posited 16 divergent-production factors in his structure-of-the-intellect model, divergent thinking is more typically treated as a single general skill. This has been especially true in divergent-thinking/creativity testing (Kagan, 1988; Treffinger, 1986; Williams, 1980). Denying the existence of general creative-thinking skills denies the importance of divergent thinking in creativity and is therefore a major challenge to most current creativity theories and methods of testing for creativity.

To provide the reader with the background of this challenge to current creativity theories, the standard divergent-thinking theory of creativity is reviewed in chapter 2, followed by an overview of the ways in which divergent-thinking theory is used in creativity testing and an introduction to some of the empirical problems that have arisen in the standard divergent-thinking model. Several modifications and reconceptualizations of divergent-thinking theory, as well as an approach to a connectionist model of creativity, are also outlined in chapter 2. These theories are offered to the reader prior to a detailed overview of evidence for the predictive validity of divergent-thinking tests in chapter 3 so that the reader can consider how the various theories might account for this evidence.

The review of available evidence regarding the validity of divergent-thinking theory in chapter 3 includes both predictive validity studies (using subjects untrained in divergent-thinking skills) and studies of the effects of training in divergent thinking. Divergent thinking is central to a variety of creativity-training programs, most of which include divergent thinking as a major component and claim considerable success in improving trainees' creative-thinking abilities (e.g., Baer, 1988b; Covington, Crutchfield, Davies, & Olton, 1974; Crabbe, 1985; Feldhusen, Treffinger, & Bahlke, 1970; Gordon, 1961; Gourley, 1981; Hoomes, 1986; Isaksen & Parnes, 1985; Micklus & Micklus, 1986; Myers & Torrance, 1964; National Talent Network, 1989; Olton & Crutchfield, 1969; Osborn, 1963; Parnes, 1972, 1985; Parnes & Noller, 1973, 1974; Perkins, 1981; Rose & Lin, 1984; Rubinstein, 1975, 1980; von Oech, 1983). Unfortunately, because most of the studies that claim to show positive effects of training in divergent thinking on creative performance have used divergent-thinking tests as their criterion measure

(Rose & Lin, 1984; Torrance & Presbury, 1984), these studies can show only that training in divergent thinking produces higher divergent-thinking test scores—they can tell us nothing about the validity of the divergent-thinking model, or whether training in divergent thinking leads to more creative performance on tasks other than divergent-thinking tests. Although there have been a few evaluations of creativity-training programs that have not relied on Torrance tests or other measures of divergent thinking (e.g., Baer, 1988b; Mansfield, Busse, & Krepelka, 1978; Olton & Crutchfield, 1969), these studies have been criticized for claiming to improve general creative-thinking ability based on test results that show only that students improved in the specific kind of problem solving taught in the course (Mansfield, Busse, & Krepelka, 1978; Mayer, 1983). An interpretation of the success of creativity training based on improvement in narrowly defined creative-performance tasks is consistent with a task-specific understanding of creative performance.

Two new studies that were designed to test the effects of training in divergent thinking on creative performance in several domains are described in detail in chapter 5. In these studies, subjects (in both cases second-grade students) were trained in divergent-thinking techniques prior to testing. As in the studies of untrained subjects reported in chapter 4, the tests consisted of a series of tasks such as writing poems and making collages. These products were then evaluated for creativity by experts in the appropriate fields. The results of these studies point to the interesting (and seemingly contradictory) conclusions that (a) divergent-thinking training does produce creativity-enhancing effects in a variety of domains, but (b) the creativity enhancement produced by divergent-thinking training is not the result of an increase in any general creativity-relevant skill, but is instead the result of increased competence in a variety of different, apparently task-specific, skills.

Chapter 6 proposes a new approach to creativity theory that divides creativity theory into two parts: (a) domain-transcending, universal theories that group skills (such as the divergent-thinking skills of fluency, flexibility, originality, and elaboration) that appear to be similar into conceptually useful categories, and (b) task-specific, particularistic theories that recognize important cognitive differences among skills that have a conceptual similarity (skills that are similar only when viewed from the "outside," as it were). As an example, a skill practiced and applied in one task domain (such as fluency in generating rhyming words) may be conceptually similar to skills in other task domains (such as fluency in generating words that are synonymous to a given word, or fluency in generating different arrangements of a given set of geometric shapes). Successful practice of one such skill will nevertheless fail to influence performance of other seemingly related skills. The skills themselves are distinct and unrelated on a cognitive level—and yet consideration of the conceptual similarity of these cognitively different skills can nonetheless help us identify skills that may be important contributors to creative performance in particular task domains. The recommendations for research, theory, and training presented in chapter 6 are based on an understanding of divergent thinking as not one, but many skills, skills that for the most part are still waiting to be identified and measured (and possibly targeted in narrowly focused, domain-specific creativity training).

The outline of the presentation, then, is as follows. In chapter 2, standard divergent-thinking theories of creativity and the role of divergent thinking in creativity testing are reviewed. Possible revisions of and replacements for the standard divergent-thinking theories of creativity are also proposed.

In chapter 3, empirical evidence of the influence of divergent thinking in creative performance is presented. Two major strands of this research—studies of the predictive validity of divergent-thinking tests and studies of the effects of training in divergent thinking—are reviewed.

In chapter 4, a review of the research I conducted of the generality of creativity across performance domains is presented. This research demonstrates that, in subjects untrained in divergent thinking, no general creative-thinking skill (such as divergent thinking) plays a significant role.

Chapter 5 focuses on two studies that were designed to test the effects of training in divergent thinking on creative performance in several domains. These studies extend to subjects with training in divergent thinking the conclusion of chapter 4 that no general creativity-relevant skills exist, while at the same time supporting claims that training in divergent thinking enhances creative performance across a variety of task domains.

The final chapter (chapter 6) summarizes the evidence reported in chapters 2–5, draws conclusions in the form of a new, two-layered approach to thinking about the nature of creativity, and offers recommendations for further research that will help us better understand creativity and improve our creativity-training efforts.

# 2

# Theories of Creativity

Any survey of theories of creativity must be selective—there are far too many different and interesting ideas about the nature of creativity to include in one book, much less one chapter—and, as a result, many important ideas and worthwhile perspectives on creativity will be omitted in what follows. The theories that are discussed in this chapter were chosen for the purposes of (a) highlighting the issues raised in chapter 1 regarding the most appropriate level(s) of specificity for theories of the cognitive mechanisms underlying creative performance, and (b) providing a frame of reference for judging the experimental data reported in chapters 3, 4, and 5. It is only fair in making such a selective review that the grounds for including (and excluding) theories be made clear at the outset. Two primary goals guided the choices I have made. First, I wanted to include some of the most popular, persistent, and therefore influential theories. Second, I wanted to present a range of theories that would highlight a continuum ranging from global, domain-transcending, all-purpose theories of creativity to limited, domain/task-specific, highly constrained models of creative performance. Readers may disagree about how well or how poorly these goals have been accomplished, but should in any event bear the goals in mind when noting particular theories or viewpoints that have been overlooked or overemphasized.

This chapter presents two kinds of theories of cognition—divergent-thinking theories (concentrating primarily on Guilford's [1956, 1967] divergent-production and Torrance's [1966, 1974, 1984, 1988, 1990] divergent-thinking theories) and associative theories (focusing primarily on Mednick's associative theory and on an application of connectionist theory to creativity). This theoretical background will help the reader assess the evidence presented in chapters 3, 4, and 5 regarding the divergent-thinking theory of creativity and the possibility of developing any useful general theory of creativity. This examination of some current creativity theories also provides the reader with a framework for approaching one of the major concerns of this book: the search for the most appropriate and productive conceptual level(s) for cognitive theories of creativity.

The proposed division of theories of creativity into divergent-thinking and associative theories will not surprise those who have followed the history of psychological thinking about creativity (see, e.g., Wallach, 1970), although some readers may wish to argue (correctly, I believe) that, in at least one important sense, associative theories (both Mednick's, 1962, theory and the connectionist approach outlined later) can be thought of as theories that explain the mechanisms underlying divergent thinking. Other readers might complain that this survey fails to include many theories of creativity that do not fit into either classification—there are certainly many such theories— or argue for the inclusion of other theories in the discussion of the two categories I have proposed; however, for the purposes of this book, only these two types of theories, and the two examples I have selected of each, will be necessary.

Those who have followed recent developments in cognitive psychology will also not be surprised to hear that a connectionist approach to creativity is being proposed, although, to my knowledge, there has not yet been any discussion (at least in print) of theories of creativity under a connectionist model of cognition. *Connectionism* (by which term I refer to all parallel distributed processing models) is one of the most hotly debated ideas in cognitive psychology, however, and it was only a matter of time until some kind of connectionist model of creativity would be suggested.

What may come as a surprise to readers familiar with both connectionism and theories of creativity is that the connectionist theory of creativity discussed later is grouped with other associative theories. Although connectionism is, basically, a way of thinking about cognition based on forming associations, the differences between a connectionist way of looking at cognition and the way of thinking about creativity that earlier associative models have offered are nonetheless enormous. Those differences should not be minimized, and I do not propose that it is less than a giant leap from Mednick's (1962) associative theory to Rumelhart and McClelland's (1986b; McClelland, Rumelhart, & the PDP Research Group, 1986; Rumelhart, McClelland, & the PDP Research Group, 1986) connectionist models. The point of relating connectionism to other associative models, however, is to begin the development of a continuum of theories of creativity, from the very low-level, nonrepresentational, minimal-assumption theory of connectionism to the much higher level theory that divergent thinking represents. This theoretical continuum provides a background for arguments that appear throughout this book (and are summarized in chapter 6) about the most productive level(s) for theories of creativity.

## DIVERGENT-THINKING THEORIES

### Divergent Production in Guilford's Structure of Intellect

One of the most popular cognitive theories of creativity is Guilford's theory of divergent production (Guilford, 1950, 1956, 1967; Guilford & Hoepfner, 1971). As noted in chapter 1, creativity has come to mean divergent thinking (as divergent production is now more commonly called) in much research in, assessment of, and theorizing about creativity (e.g., Crockenberg, 1972; Hattie, 1980; Heausler & Thompson, 1988; Kagan, 1988; Kaplan, 1990; Kogan, 1983; Mayer, 1983; Mc-Crae, Arenberg, & Costa, 1987; Rose & Lin, 1984; Runco, 1986b; Torrance, 1972b, 1984, 1990; Torrance & Presbury, 1984; Treffinger, 1986; Wallace, Goldstein, & Nathan, 1990; Wallach, 1970; Wallach & Kogan, 1965a, 1965b).

Divergent production is part of Guilford's structure-of-intellect model, an attempt to organize all of human cognition along three dimensions: (a) thought processes, or operations, that can be performed; (b) contents to which the operations can be applied; and (c) products that might result from performing operations on different content categories. These combined to produce 120 different mental abilities, many of which Guilford and his associates devised tests to measure and to demonstrate via factor analysis (Guilford, 1956, 1967; Guilford & Hoepfner, 1971).

Prior to Guilford's extensive factor analytic work, the debate about the number of factors needed to explain intelligence had focused on single-factor theories versus models that posited small numbers of factors. For example, Spearman (1927) collected individuals' scores on many different tests and looked for correlations among them. Based on his analyses, he proposed a two-factor theory of intelligence, with a general factor operating across domains and other domain-specific skills contributing to intelligent performance only on domain-relevant tasks. Among theories of creativity, Amabile's (1983, p. 67) "componential" model transfers these two factors into a theory of creativity as general "creativity-relevant" skills and specific "domain-relevant" skills, plus a third component of "task motivation."

Thurstone (1938) modified Spearman's statistical technique somewhat and found seven "primary mental abilities": verbal comprehension, numerical fluency, associative memory, perceptual speed, spatial visualization, verbal fluency, and inductive reasoning. Guilford's proposal of 120 distinct mental abilities was a large quantitative leap based on a conceptual, qualitative break with his predecessors. He argued for a broad view of intelligence, complaining that "certain kinds of tests have been favored in intelligence scales. Unfortunately, ... the concept of intelligence became circumscribed within the limits of such collections of tests" (Guilford, 1967, p. 37). He agreed with Boring's (1923) contention that intelligence becomes whatever the intelligence tests test, and lamented the narrow range of abilities being assessed on such tests.

One reason why Guilford—using factor-analytic techniques similar to the ones Spearman (1927) and Thurstone (1938) had employed—found so many more distinct factors was his inclusion of questions to tap divergent thinking—or, as he called it, divergent-production ability (Guilford, 1967). These questions had no single correct answer; for example, "Imagine all the things that would happen if all national and local laws were suddenly abolished," or "Name as many uses as you can think of for a toothpick" (Darley, Glucksberg, & Kinchla, 1986, p. 339.)

Guilford fought against "the very popular conception that intelligence is learning ability and that it is a universal ability" (Guilford, 1967, p. 20). In defending his 120-factor model, Guilford argued that there is no such thing as general intelligence. People can be very good or very bad at any combination of different components of intelligence. His 120 factors are not hierarchically organized, but neither are they entirely independent of one another: in his morphological model, each cell has equal status with every other cell, but some pairs (and larger groups) of cells are related to one another, whereas other pairs are entirely unrelated. Thus all of the factors that come about via divergent production are linked to one another, and distinct from factors that are produced via one of the other four operations (convergent production, cognition, memory, and evaluation). The divergent-production factors themselves differ in their contents (figural, symbolic, semantic, and behavioral) and their products (units, classes, relations, systems, transformations, and implications).

Although there is a strong empirical flavor to the hypotheses that initially guided his research (Guilford, 1950, 1967), the five-operations-times-four-contents-times-six-products model led Guilford to develop tests to find some hypothesized skills in the 120-factor matrix that were far from empirically obvious. Inventing tests for these diverse factors was a task requiring considerable imagination, and Guilford and Hoepfner's (1971) Appendix B "Tests Employed by the Aptitudes Research Project in Its Analysis of Intelligence" contains some of the most unusual tests to be found anywhere in the psychometric literature.

The full structure-of-intellect model is still used by some psychologists and educators (especially in the work of the Structure of Intellect Institute; see also Meeker, 1969, 1985; and Smith, Michael, & Hocevar, 1990), but simplified versions of the theory in which several factors have been collapsed into one, such as those in which the various divergent-production factors are grouped either as a single skill, or as a set of just a few related skills, have become more common. Guilford correctly noted that "of all the investigations in any area by the ARP [Aptitudes Research Project], those aimed at creative abilities have been rewarded with the most novel results, have been given the most attention, and have had the most consequences in the form of stimulating thinking and research by others" (Guilford & Hoepfner, 1971, p. 123). However, the divergent-production theory to which he referred has been modified considerably by those who have inherited it.

## Descendents of Guilford: Divergent-Thinking Theories of Creativity

Guilford (1967) grouped the 16 divergent-production factors that he initially was able to identify into four categories:

1. Fluency (which includes word fluency, ideational fluency, associationistic fluency, and expressional fluency) is the ability to produce a large number of ideas.
2. Flexibility is the ability to produce a wide variety of ideas.
3. Originality is the ability to produce unusual ideas.
4. Elaboration is the ability to develop or embellish ideas, and to produce many details to "flesh out" an idea.

Depending on the kind of thinking task to which divergent production is to be applied (e.g., verbal as opposed to figural), Guilford described different kinds of divergent thinking. This distinction between different kinds of divergent thinking has, however, been largely ignored in many theories of creativity, and divergent thinking is typically thought of as a single, all-purpose, creativity-relevant skill. This has often been the case in divergent-thinking/creativity testing, in which a single creativity score is reported (Kagan, 1988; Treffinger, 1986; Williams, 1980). Moreover, even in cases where the distinction between different types of divergent thinking has been retained in the form of subtests, there are often methods for summing the several subtest scores into a total creativity score (Heausler & Thompson, 1988; Thorndike, 1972; Torrance, 1990).

Guilford's (1967) original conceptualization of divergent thinking has been retained in current creativity theorizing primarily in the 4 general categories into which he grouped them (fluency, flexibility, originality, and elaboration), not in the 16 divergent-production factors that he identified or the 24 such factors that his theory posited (Kogan, 1983; Torrance, 1990; Wallach, 1970). This is the case of the most influential divergent-thinking theory of creativity, that of E. Paul Torrance (Torrance, 1966, 1972b, 1984, 1988, 1990). The influence of Torrance's theory derives primarily from the success of his tests of creativity. According to one comprehensive survey of creativity research (Torrance & Presbury, 1984), the Torrance tests were used in three-quarters of all recently published studies of creativity involving elementary- and secondary-school students, and 40% of all creativity studies with college students and adults. The Torrance tests dominate the field of creativity research to such an extent that, in what was intended as a comprehensive meta-analytic evaluation of the long-term effects of various creativity training programs, only studies that employed the Torrance tests were included (Rose & Lin, 1984).

Torrance's original tests provide separate fluency, flexibility, originality, and elaboration scores, as well as an overall creativity index (Torrance, 1966). The most recent scoring system (Torrance, 1990), although more complex, is not a major theoretical departure from earlier systems. These scores can be used separately, as measures of the component skills of divergent thinking, or combined into an overall divergent-thinking index score. Torrance mildly discouraged the use of a composite score, recommending instead that the subscales be interpreted "in relation to one another" (Torrance, 1974, pp. 56–57). There is considerable evidence that the subscale scores are highly intercorrelated, however. Factor-analytic studies do not support the view that the subscales yield discrete scores (Borland, 1986; Heausler & Thompson, 1988; Hocevar, 1979; Runco, 1986a). In a survey of available evidence, Kogan (1983) reported that fluency scores (which measure only the quantity of responses) and the other "quality" scores (including flexibility, originality, and elaboration) correlate so highly that "a strong case can obviously be made for exclusive reliance on the more easily scorable ideational-fluency index" (p. 637). Other authors' criticisms of the subscales extend to the entire test: "It should be evident that use of more than a single score from the Torrance battery makes little sense, and that the major question still unanswered is whether, or, put more optimistically, in what context it makes sense to use a score from the Torrance battery at all" (Oon-Chye & Bridgham, 1971, p. 4).

There is still debate about whether these tests measure several divergent-thinking skills or just one general divergent-thinking skill. Despite this uncertainty, the widespread use of the Torrance Tests of Creative Thinking have led scores on these tests to become the de facto operational definition (or definitions, if subscale scores are used) of divergent thinking. There is an even more crucial uncertainty about the Torrance tests, however, that focuses on their validity as measures of creativity, as will be shown later (primarily in chapter 3, with additional evidence presented in chapters 4 and 5).

### Separating Performance and Competence: A Metacognitive Approach to the Divergent-Thinking Theories of Creativity

The influence of any skill on actual performance involves at least two conceptually distinct factors: availability and production. One must have the skill available, of course, or it cannot be produced; but it is possible not to produce a skill in appropriate situations even though that skill is available, which would make it appear (falsely) that one lacks the skill in question. This distinction between availability and production, or between competence and performance, is a common one (e.g., Brown, Bransford, Ferrara, & Campione, 1983; Flavell, 1970, 1985; Flavell & Wellman, 1977; Kaplan, 1990; Mayer, 1987), but it has not been applied to the hypothesized influence of divergent thinking on creative performance.

The distinction between skill availability and skill production is part of the "fashionable but complex" (Brown et al., 1983, p. 106) realm of metacognition. Brown et al., although acknowledging the importance of many of the skills that have been labeled metacognitive (and in fact arguing that these skills are often not optional "extra's," but skills that are central to learning), described metacognition as "not only a monster of obscure parentage, but also a many-headed monster at that" (p. 124). There is disagreement about whether it is productive to group together as metacognitive (a) diverse categories of knowledge about people, tasks, and strategies relevant to cognition; (b) many varieties of strategic control, including the distinctions necessary to reflect the particular skills and knowledge that they control; and (c) skills that involve different levels of conscious and unconscious processing. That is, should metacognition be considered as a family of related skills or as an unrelated set of skills that influence cognition? (For opposing viewpoints, see Brown et al., 1983; and Flavell, 1985.) Despite this controversy, however, it is widely believed that many of the skills that currently share the label *metacognitive* are important thinking skills. Furthermore, the distinction between skill availability and skill production appears to be a useful one, especially in regard to memory strategies (see, e.g., Bjorklund, 1985; Flavell, 1970, 1985; Glass & Holyoak, 1986; Hagen & Stanovich, 1977; Kail & Siegel, 1977; Lange, 1978; Ornstein, Baker-Ward, & Naus, 1988 Ornstein & Naus, 1978; Ornstein, Naus, & Stone, 1977; Smiley & Brown, 1979) and reading comprehension (see, e.g., Brown, Campione,

& Barclay, 1979; Flavell, 1985; Garner & Reis, 1981; Markman, 1985).

An important distinction must be made between divergent-thinking skill and mnemonic skills like specific rehearsal strategies, however. In many cases, it is possible to simply instruct subjects to employ a rehearsal strategy, such as repeating aloud a set of items to be recalled later (e.g., Ornstein et al., 1977), and the use of such a strategy can be clearly observed. In the case of many mnemonic skills and strategies, it is possible that a subject either has the skill or does not have it; it is possible that one might either apply or not apply the skill; and it is even possible, in some cases, to monitor such application directly (leaving aside the issues of how such overt actions like saying words aloud might be different from silent rehearsal, and the degree of automaticity typical in the routine application of such skills).

Application of divergent-thinking skill, on the other hand, is much less dichotomous and much less easily monitored. One might possess and use varying amounts of divergent-thinking skill. One might also apply such skill in a variety of ways to the same task. Furthermore, in most cases, one cannot observe, but only infer, that such skill has been applied. Put another way, one might say that divergent-thinking skill is less well-defined than many of the mnemonic strategies that have been studied. Clearly, divergent-thinking skill is not directly comparable to a mnemonic skill such as rehearsal or organization.

If, however, it is possible that divergent-thinking skill can be present but not employed at appropriate times—and there is no a priori reason that this could not be the case—then it is possible that, because students (or, for that matter, adults) have not been trained to use divergent thinking in creativity-relevant situations, this skill may have little effect on their creative performance. Divergent thinking is not a discrete skill that one learns at a particular point in time, a skill that one either possesses or lacks entirely. Everyone has some degree of divergent-thinking skill. But because it is neither commonly taught nor generally recognized by most children and adults as an important creative-thinking skill, production deficiencies—failures to use divergent thinking at times when it would be an effective strategy—may be common. A revised divergent-thinking theory of creativity might thus argue that knowing when to apply divergent-thinking skill is at least as important as the degree to which one has the skill available.

Everyone has some measure of divergent-thinking skill; furthermore, this skill—as measured by the Torrance Tests of Creative Thinking—is easily improved with practice. In fact, simply altering the test instructions to encourage a different kind of responding can result in significant improvements in divergent-thinking test scores, without any training whatsoever (Lissitz & Willhoft, 1985). Knowing when to apply divergent thinking (in creativity-relevant situations) may be even more important than the degree of divergent-thinking skill available. Put differently, production deficiencies in divergent thinking may limit creative thinking more than deficiencies in the availability of divergent-thinking skill. This would be the principal distinction between this revised divergent-thinking theory of creativity and the standard divergent-thinking theory.

This distinction between availability and production of divergent thinking, if verified, might allow divergent thinking a role in creative performance, albeit a reduced one, despite the evidence (discussed in detail in chapter 4) that no general creative thinking skill like divergent thinking plays a significant role in the creative performance of subjects untrained in divergent thinking. In particular, it could account for alleged improvements in performance resulting from training in the use of divergent thinking. Although creativity-training programs typically try to improve the availability of divergent-thinking skill, in doing so they also teach its application (Baer, 1988b; Covington, Crutchfield, Davies, & Olton, 1974; Crabbe, 1985; Feldhusen, Treffinger, & Bahlke, 1970; Gordon, 1961; Gourley, 1981; Hoomes, 1986; Isaksen & Parnes, 1985; Mayer, 1983, 1987; Micklus & Micklus, 1986; Myers & Torrance, 1964; National Talent Network, 1989; Olton & Crutchfield, 1969; Osborn, 1963; Parnes, 1972, 1985; Parnes & Noller, 1973, 1974; Perkins, 1981; Rose & Lin, 1984; Rubinstein, 1975, 1980; von Oech, 1983). If such training can be demonstrated to cause general improvement in creative performance, a revised divergent-thinking theory of creativity would be one way to account for such an effect.

## ASSOCIATIVE THEORIES OF CREATIVITY

Perhaps the most influential associative theory of creativity is the one outlined in Mednick's (1962) "The Associative Basis of the Creative Process" and operationalized in Mednick and Mednick's (1967) *Remote Associates Test*. Mednick's introduction to his theory —the first two paragraphs of his 1962 article in *Psychological Review*—tell us a great deal about the goals and methods of his work:

> The intent of this paper is the presentation of an associative interpretation of the process of creative thinking. The explanation is not directed to any specific field of application such as art or science but attempts to delineate the processes that underlie all creative thought.
>
> The discussion will take the following form. (a) First, we will define creative thinking in associative terms and indicate three ways in which creative solutions may be achieved—serendipity, similarity, and mediation. (b) This definition will allow us to deduce those individual difference variables which will facilitate creative performance. (c) Consideration of the definition of the creative process has suggested an operational statement in the form of a test. The test will be briefly described along with some preliminary research results. (d) The paper will conclude with a discussion of predictions regarding the influence of certain experimentally manipulable variables upon the creative process. (Mednick, 1962, p. 220)

Mednick made it quite clear from the outset that he was looking for a general, domain-transcending theory that would account equally well for creativity no matter what the task domain. His orientation was clearly theoretical: He not only assumed that such general approaches would work, but also that such theory building could be accomplished by definition and logic and followed by empirical confirmation, but neither guided nor constrained in its conception by empirical data.

In a very important sense, the divergent-thinking theories of Guilford (1956,

1967) and Torrance (1966, 1974, 1984, 1988, 1990) described earlier are also associationistic, in that both use as estimates of divergent-thinking ability (and therefore creativity) the number and diversity of ideas that come to mind in response to (or that one associates with) some cue. Mednick's (1962) theory was certainly influenced by Guilford's (1956) earlier work, although Guilford is not cited in Mednick's paper. It seems almost as if Mednick set himself the task of explaining how the ideas that result from divergent thinking come to be produced, and also how such ideas are selected (although, like Guilford and almost everyone else who has worked in this field [Runco, 1991b], he was apparently much less interested in the evaluation of ideas than in their production).

In contrast, connectionism, although clearly based on a theory of association among cognitive elements, was not developed to explain either divergent production or creativity, but rather as a comprehensive theory of all cognition. It is a theory unlike any other in psychology today. In contrast to associationistic theories conceived to account for creative thinking, including those of Mednick (1962), Maltzman and his collaborators (Maltzman, 1960; Maltzman, Belloni, & Fishbein, 1964; Maltzman, Bogartz, & Breger, 1958; Maltzman, Brooks, Bogartz, & Summers, 1958; Maltzman, Simon, Raskin, & Licht, 1960), and Wallach and Kogan (1965a, 1965b), connectionism does not have ideas, concepts, or even words as its most basic units. The cognitive elements that are associated—or connected—in connectionism are typically at a level below, or occurring prior to, the emergence of any interpretable meaning. As such, these associations may simply be the basis for higher level constructs (such as words, concepts, or ideas) that have associative lives of their own. Conversely, the seemingly almost neural level at which these associations occur may be the highest cognitive level at which any cognitively important associations occur, and analysis at any higher level may mislead us to ascribe causality where none exists and to mistake psychological metaphors describing cognitive processes for the actual agents of cognition. It is under this most radical interpretation that connectionism is most interesting, and it is only connectionism at or near this most basic level that provides a serious challenge to all higher order theories of cognition. The extreme case will be argued later to provide one endpoint for a continuum of possible levels at which we might attempt to build a cognitive psychology of creativity, with theories of divergent thinking well along toward the opposite end, and Mednick's associative theory somewhere in between.

## Mednick's Associative Theory of Creative Thought

Fifty years before Mednick conceived his theory of creativity, the French mathematician Poincare anticipated its essential elements when he wrote, "To create consists of making new combinations of associative elements which are useful. ... Among chosen combinations the most fertile will often be those formed of elements drawn from domains which are far apart" (quoted by Mednick, 1962, pp. 220–221). Mednick's definition of creativity—and the starting point of his theory—is an almost exact paraphrase of Poincare. Mednick's theory of creative thinking, as

Mednick (1962) was quick to point out, is also similar to ideas advanced by many British associationists from Locke to Bain, and by Freud, Hollingsworth, and Binet.

Mednick argued that any condition that increases the likelihood of bringing together the associative elements needed for a creative solution will increase the probability of that creative solution being discovered. He proposed three ways this might happen.

"Serendipity" refers to any chance contiguity of associative elements in the environment that leads one to a creative insight. "Similarity" of associative elements or of the stimuli that evoke those elements is a second route by which associations may occur. "Mediation" of common elements, typically through the use of symbols, is the third process that leads to creative associations.

There are individual differences in the probability of discovering or producing creative solutions, and Mednick (1962) advanced five factors that may account for these differences:

1. Domain-specific knowledge is essential—one cannot use a requisite element in a creative solution if one is not aware of the existence of that element —although such knowledge can also impede creative associations due to overlearning of common or "correct" associations, which makes it less likely that one will make an association employing a remote element to produce a creative solution.

2. Some people produce greater numbers of associations, thereby increasing the likelihood of a creative solution being achieved. Mednick argued that what is important is the total number of associations that one makes, not the speed at which they are produced.

3. Differences in cognitive or personality style, whether innate or learned, may influence the probability of reaching a creative solution. Mednick noted that he defines these variables rather poorly (the two examples he gave are perceptual vs. conceptual approaches to problem solving, and visualizer vs. verbalizer styles of thinking). It is among the variables that constitute this factor that he suggested might be found the reasons for different individual aptitudes for creative performance in different task domains.

4. The selection of the creative combination from the many possible associations is central to a theory of creativity, and Mednick acknowledged its importance. He did not, however, develop this part of the theory, as noted earlier.

5. The most important factor of the five Mednick proposed, and the one that has generated the most research, is what he termed the *associative hierarchy*. This refers to how an individual's associations are organized. Important in this regard is the pattern of relative strengths of the various associations one has to a given concept. (See Fig. 2.1.) Among less creative people, the associative hierarchy is steep, with a few ideas that have a very high probability of being produced and a very low probability of producing other ideas. More creative people have flatter associative hierarchies, with more nearly equal probability of making a large number of associations. This increases the likelihood of less common associations—associations between elements that are more remote, and therefore more likely to lead to creative solutions. Another type of associative hierarchy that leads

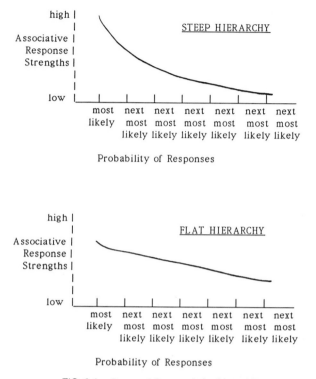

FIG. 2.1. Steep and flat associative hierarchies.

to creative solutions, Mednick argued, is a steep but deviant hierarchy, in which one may have only a few very dominant associative responses, but ones that are unlike the dominant associations of other people.

With the exceptions of cognitive style factors and differences in domain-specific knowledge, these factors are expected to influence one's likelihood of producing creative associations (and, therefore, of demonstrating creative thought and behavior) in all tasks equally. In the case of response hierarchies, for example, Mednick did not propose that a person has a unique hierarchy for every element in his or her cognitive repertoire (although this would probably be how psychologists familiar with spreading activation networks would envision this model today). In order for this to be a general theory of creativity, however, any elaboration of Mednick's theory must at least argue that people have general tendencies to organize their associative hierarchies in a particular way (e.g., in regard to steepness).

Mednick and Mednick (1967) developed the Remote Associates Test (RAT) as a means of assessing individual differences in creativity. Although it did not have the wide-ranging impact of divergent-thinking tests like the Torrance Tests of Creativity (Rose & Lin, 1984; Torrance, 1966, 1990; Torrance & Presbury,

1984), a brief examination of the test will nonetheless be useful in trying to understand Mednick's theory and the assumptions on which it is based.

Each item on the test consists of three words, such as:

cookies        sixteen        heart

The task is to find a fourth word that is related to all three words. In this case, "sweet" is the answer (Mednick & Mednick, 1967).

Another example:

out        dog        cat

The answer is "house" (Mednick, 1962).

One's score is the sum of all correct responses. The test is timed.

In devising the RAT, Mednick (1962) confronted the problem of domain-specific knowledge:

> If a test is to be appropriate for all fields of creative endeavor, the material must either be nonsensical so as to avoid bias favoring any specific means of creative expression, or it must be so common in society that familiarity could be assumed to be high across fields of interest. The problems involved in constructing the nonsense materials so as to avoid favoring any interest group soon proved to be insurmountable. This left us searching for materials with which most individuals in the culture could claim acquaintance; this, in turn, brought us to verbal materials. (p. 227)

Mednick (1962) acknowledged that some groups may have more extensive knowledge of and experience dealing with words, but assumed that almost all people brought up in the United States would have similar linguistic backgrounds and associative bonds. The total implausibility of this assumption need not concern us, even though it casts serious doubt on the possibility of the test having even a modicum of validity when used with diverse groups, because it is the validity of the theory, not the test, that is our focus. Whether or not the RAT is an effective assessment device, the theory upon which it is based maintains that general, domain-transcending cognitive processes are important in creative performance. This is the assumption that much of the research reported in chapters 4 and 5 calls into question. It is also a perspective that has been integrated into the metatheory of creativity that is elaborated in chapter 6.

As suggested earlier, it is possible for one theory of creativity to be the substrate that supports another theory of creativity. Mednick's analysis of the ways that creative associations are formed, and in particular his hypothesis regarding the organization of response hierarchies, could be thought of as a theory of the processes underlying divergent thinking. That is, it may be that divergent thinking skills rely, to a significant degree, on the kinds of associations one makes, and that these associations in turn depend on the general organization of one's response hierarchies. If this is the case, then one must ask whether both levels of analysis are useful, or if one level or the other is redundant. If, for example, almost all differences in individual divergent-thinking skill could be accounted for by differences in how those individuals make associations among cognitive elements, then analysis at the level of divergent thinking would be superfluous. If, on the other hand, differences in how individuals make associations could account for only some of the differences in their divergent-thinking skills, and if both factors could be shown to be important contributors to creative performance, then both levels of analysis might be important. Finally, if differences in how individuals form associations could account for only a very small portion of the differences in their creative performance, then analyses of their associative hierarchies—and consideration of the other factors proposed by Mednick's theory—would be of little value.

## A CONNECTIONIST APPROACH TO CREATIVITY

Connectionist models of cognition, also known as parallel distributed-processing or neural-network models, have recently challenged traditional symbol-processing cognitive models in many arenas (P. M. Churchland, 1988; P. S. Churchland, 1989; Johnson-Laird, 1988a; McClelland, Rumelhart, & the PDP Research Group, 1986; Pinker & Prince, 1987; Rumelhart, McClelland, & the PDP Research Group, 1986; Smolensky, 1988). This section begins by explaining the theoretical claims of connectionist models in general. Readers who are familiar with the connectionist paradigm, as well as those who are willing to accept the implications of connectionist models without wrestling with the details of those models, may wish to skip this explanation.

### The Philosophy and Methodology of Connectionism

There are two principle "stories" in cognitive science today, two ways of explaining cognition in general. One such account is the rule-based model that heeds the "central dogma" (Pinker & Prince, 1987, p. 2) of classical cognitive science—that intelligence results from the manipulation of symbolic expressions—and that argues the necessity of explicit, though often inaccessible, rules at all significant levels of cognition. The other is the connectionist paradigm that maintains that what appears to be lawful cognitive behavior may in fact be produced by a mechanism in which symbolic representations are unnecessary, and in which no rules are "written in explicit form anywhere in the mechanism" (Rumelhart & McClelland, 1986b).

Let me first explain what is not the single most important "key" to understanding connectionism, although the popular press sometimes claims it to be: Connectionist systems are based on parallel rather than serial processing. Although it is true that most nonconnectionist (i.e., symbol-manipulation) computer simulations of human cognition have employed serial (one-step-at-a-time) computers, this has been in part simply a matter of convenience. Parallel- and serial-processing computers can in fact mimic the performance of one another (if the time dimension is ignored—

appropriately programmed parallel processors are much faster because they carry out many operations at the same time, in contrast to the one-at-a-time bottleneck of a serial computer's central processing unit). Serial computers have been much more readily available, and have therefore been used to simulate both serial and parallel models of human cognition. Production systems, for example, though often implemented on serial computers that search one-by-one for matching conditions, typically assume that such searching is actually done in a single parallel step in human brains. Because connectionist models do employ parallel processing on a tremendous scale—and because parallel processing is a significant requirement of a connectionist system, even though such a system can be simulated on a serial computer—this difference has sometimes been mistakenly focused on as their defining feature. The central issue dividing connectionism and the information-processing, representational view of the mind is not, however, simply one of serial versus parallel architecture.

According to the standard view in modern cognitive science, cognition consists of rules and symbols, on one hand, and elementary symbol-processing mechanisms, on the other (all made possible in some undefined way by neural tissue). It has been demonstrated that a universal Turing machine (a conceptually very primitive information-processing device with an infinitely long coded tape that contains a program and a description of the current state of the machine) can simulate the operations of any particular computer, and thus, with appropriate modifications, any software can be made to run on any suitably powerful computer (Johnson-Laird, 1988a). Cognitive science has used computers to model human cognition on the assumption that while searching for the proper software (i.e., software that will faithfully mimic human performance), the question of hardware implementation (silicon vs. carbon) could be safely ignored (see, e.g., Baer, 1988a; Dennett, 1986, 1991; Gardner, 1985; Hofstadter, 1985; see Searle, 1980, for an opposing point of view).

Some cognitive models have been greatly influenced by the computers on which they have been implemented, however, reflecting more the history of computer design than psychologically motivated constraints. The brain is generally much slower and messier than electronic computers, and this puts limitations on which symbol-manipulating abilities the brain can supply "for free"—as an inherent part of its natural functioning—and which must be composed of more primitive processes.

Connectionism arose partly in response to a perceived need to work with computer hardware that more faithfully mimics the principles and capacities of the brain. The distinction between hardware and software vanishes in the connectionist paradigm, as there is no "intelligence" (i.e., software) in the system other than the physical operating features of the system itself. The individual primitive units of a connectionist computer—dubbed "subsymbols" by Smolensky (1988, p. 3)—are each connected with large numbers of similar primitive units, making it a massively parallel, densely interconnected machine. These units, or subsymbols, are not operated on by symbolic manipulation, but "participate in only numeric—not symbolic—computation" (Smolensky, 1988, p. 3). The units have no semantic content, but they all have individual activation levels, and they transmit signals (with strength proportional to their activation levels) to one another along weighted connections. The weights of these connections are "learned"—that is, they are modified during training—and the signal that is passed along any connection is a function of both the activation level of the sending unit and the current strength of the connection. Activation levels are constantly changing, depending on the individual unit's input, and output from any unit occurs when it reaches its individual threshold.

Although it will have no impact on the case being argued here, it should be noted in passing that at least one prominent neuroscientist, Gerald Edelman (1987, 1989), complained that connectionism is still too closely tied to an information-processing way of thinking to be an adequate model of human cognition. Edelman claimed that connectionist models "do not avoid the difficulties of the information-processing approach, inasmuch as they require specification of both input and output of a system" (1989, p. 282). Edelman may well be right, which would mean that one endpoint of the continuum I have proposed may need to be pushed still further in the direction of task-specificity and lower level processes. For the purpose of establishing this continuum of lower-to-higher-level cognitive processors, however, we need not worry about the exact location of the endpoints, or just how low or high are the anchors used to define it.

## Hidden Units

Key to understanding connectionist architecture are "hidden units"—units that are neither input nor output units, and which, unlike the intermediate states of computation in symbolic accounts, represent noninterpretable states of the system. That is, these hidden units individually cannot be expressed in the form of propositions or rules, nor can their patterns of connections and interactions be expressed in rules or propositions. In less formal language, this is the same as saying that the "meanings" of these units and their various combinations cannot be stated in words or sentences.

In contrast to a system employing hidden intermediate units, if input units and output units are connected directly to one another (such as was posited in traditional associationistic—i.e., behaviorist—psychology), then the associations thus formed can make no use of either internal representations (an information-processing approach) or undefinable internal states (a connectionist approach). They can compute varying output based on varying input, but only in a most straightforward manner. Such finite-state devices require no working memory; they need only a program that turns input into output via algorithmic procedures.

Input and output can also be modulated by rules (again, an information-processing approach) that yield intermediate states that the system must hold temporarily in memory for later processing, as is the case with production systems, most computer programs, and almost all cognitive and linguistic theories. Such intermediate states have representational content —that is, they can be translated into comprehensible propositions. But in a connectionist network, there are no rules, and no intermediate states that can be expressed as propositions. There are, however, one or more layers of interconnected hidden units between input and output, and these hidden layers modulate input–output relationships. These hidden units also form a kind of memory, but one that cannot be interpreted in the form of comprehensible propositions.

Two layers of hidden units are shown in Fig. 2.2. For the purpose of explanation, this model is much more simple and orderly than an actual network would be, but the operating principles are the same. Each input unit is connected (in this example) to every unit in the first hidden layer; each of these is connected to every unit in the second hidden layer; and each of these, in turn, is connected to every output unit. In this model, the final set of connections is not adjustable. The purpose of this last layer of connections is to change the pattern associator's output into some form more suitable for human use (via an algorithmic procedure), but this is not an intrinsic part of the pattern associator. Although not shown in Fig. 2.2, there is often such a translator on the input side as well.

When an input unit is activated, it sends signals along each of its connections with the units of hidden layer 1. The strength of each of these signals will be a function of (a) the strength of the input signal, and (b) the weight of the connection. If there is only one active input unit, what each of the units in hidden layer 1 does will be determined directly by these two factors. The units may reach threshold (and send activation to the next layer of hidden inputs) or they may not. Even with a single input, tracing the input to the units of the second hidden layer gets quite complex, but the principle is the same; and so on to the output. If more than one input unit is active, of course, the story gets quite complex right from the start, with the activation level of each hidden unit computed as the sum of its input from all the active units to which it is connected.

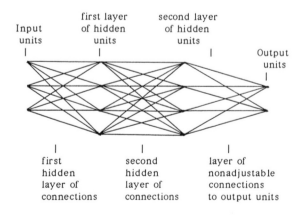

FIG. 2.2.   Schematic of a simplified connectionist system. Each layer might actually include many thousands of units.

## How Learning Occurs

In the most basic training paradigm, initial connection weights are set either at zero or at random, and are changed depending on how the output compares to the "correct" output. Over a series of runs, the system does not learn specific input–output connections (as it would without the hidden layers), nor is it controlled by a set of rules stating what to do with any given input (as it would if it were an information-processing program such as a production system), but instead it learns how to respond to any kind of input, based on the sum of the system's experiences with similar stimuli. Novel inputs or combinations of inputs will also produce outputs, based not on any explicit rule, but based very much on the results of the training runs. Much more complex (but nonsymbolic) procedures for judging outputs, based, perhaps, on the current configuration of the entire system (i.e., all that the system "knows," although at a nonrepresentational level), would, in the kind of thinking of interest to a theory of creativity, take the place of the "correct" output of the basic training paradigm in causing adjustments of connection weights.

Although learning is distributed widely throughout a connectionist system—which, like the brain, is remarkably plastic and able to function despite losses of large numbers of cells—it would be misleading to suggest that learning on any given kind of task is distributed equally throughout the system. Similar inputs will activate similar assortments of units, and different inputs will lead to different patterns of activation. Experience with one kind of task will typically have little or no impact on learning of unrelated tasks—even though both tasks may employ many of the same units, but in different patterns of connections and activations.

## "Weak" Versus "Strong" Connectionism

How faithfully a connectionist computer models the brain's hardware is a subject of some dispute, but in at least some respects (such as the subsymbolic level at which it operates and the massively parallel design) it seems closer to brain functioning than a typical von Neumann computer. It is quite possible that these differences are superfluous to questions about how human minds work, however, or how this architecture relates to the kinds of theories that have been spun using the metaphorical thread of symbol- and rule-based production systems. One possibility is that connectionism is simply a way to implement production systems, and that the learning that takes place in a connectionist system is an induction of rules, which, although not stated formally as rules, nonetheless operate on inputs in the same way that rules in a production system operate on symbols. The set of weights that the system learns, in this "weak" connectionist scenario, would simply be the program's coding of the "explicit inexpressible rules" (Rumelhart & McClelland, 1986b, p. 217) of which many connectionist theorists are trying to rid psychology. In such a weak connectionist system, relationships among collections of the hidden units would correspond to rules and representations, and the way the overall output of one connectionist network feeds into the input of another would be isomorphic to the structure of the symbol manipulations captured in statements of the rules of a production system (Pinker & Prince, 1988).

There is nothing revolutionary about this: Weak connectionism upsets few apple carts. Accepting this version of the model would imply only that connectionist systems occupy an intermediate level between the representational level and the level of neural hardware—a translator, one might call it—and this would have little direct impact on the symbol-processing concerns of cognitive psychology in general or of creativity theory in particular. There is no dispute between symbol-processing theories of mind and a connectionism seen simply as a way to implement production systems, although some revisions might be necessary in traditional models regarding the nature of primitive mechanisms.

It is also possible, however, that connectionist models may replace existing symbol-processing models as explanations of cognitive processing. This is the extreme claim of many connectionists, and it is this claim ("strong" connectionism) that has caused the most interest and controversy (P. M. Churchland, 1988; P. S. Churchland, 1989; Pinker & Prince, 1988; Smolensky, 1988). If it were not possible to find a principled mapping between an implemented connectionist system and the rule-governed symbol manipulations of a symbolic model, and if the connectionist model could account as well as the symbolic model for empirical outcomes, then there would no reason to retain ghostly symbols that no longer stood for anything real, but represented only descriptive approximations of observations in which they (the rules and symbols) had no part to play. This is the stance of "eliminative materialists" such as Paul Churchland, who suggested that "our common-sense psychological framework is a false and radically misleading conception of the causes of human behavior and the nature of cognitive activity" (P. M. Churchland, 1988, p. 43). Pinker and Prince (1988) termed this strong connectionist claim *eliminative connectionism* (1988, p. 6). Both their term and Churchland's reflect the elimination of a level—the representational level—that both folk psychology and information-processing approaches in cognitive science take as foundational. Connectionism is not, incidentally, the only possible scenario in which eliminative materialism could be shown to be true, but it is certainly the prime candidate at this time.

There are, of course, diverse intermediate positions between eliminative connectionism and connectionism as a way to instantiate symbol-manipulating systems (see, e.g., Miikkulainen & Dyer, 1991; Minsky, 1986), but it is the claim of eliminative connectionism that is of greatest interest to cognitive psychology and to creativity theory. As long as the representational view of cognition is not challenged, cognitive psychologists can go about their business as before, hoping that connectionist models will provide new insights and ways to modify theories, but safe in the knowledge that the foundation of their enterprise is secure. If the symbolic paradigm is repudiated, however, it will require a complete reworking of the theories and models of cognitive psychology—if there is still a need for such theories at all.

## A Connectionist Approach to a Theory of Creativity

Connectionism was not developed as a theory of creativity, or of any other specific subcategory of cognition. If the claims of strong or eliminative connectionism are true, then connectionism is equally a theory of collage-making creativity, of memory for names of acquaintances, of skill in rhyming words, of categorization of visual stimuli, and of how children learn to pronounce words in a language—that is, of all cognitive activity. Those who embrace eliminative connectionism allow that there is much work to be done in finding ways to simulate such subcategories of cognition: Such simulations would both demonstrate the efficacy of a connectionist approach and present the only models or theories of these subcategories of cognition that would be needed. Eliminative connectionism maintains that in regard to these subcategories (or to any superordinate categories we might imagine to unite two or more of those subcategories) there is simply little or nothing worth doing in the way of theory building of the more typical, information-processing kind. A theory of creativity for a given task (or, if it proves possible, for a larger domain of tasks) can be no more than one or several simulations of creative performance on that task, accompanied, perhaps, by arguments regarding the plausibility of a given simulation given what is known about the brain.

If, on the other hand, connectionism is true only in the weakest sense—if connectionism is important only to an analysis of cognition at an intermediate level between neurons and synapses, on the one hand, and representations and rules, on the other—then it is of little importance in developing a cognitive theory of creativity. One could acknowledge its underlying importance in the same way one recognizes the importance of the brain's neural hardware, while nonetheless continuing, in effect, to ignore it completely. Under a weak connectionist scenario, connectionism merely helps to explain how the representational level comes to be—how the level of meaningful symbols and rules to manipulate those symbols emerges from the activity of neurons and synapses. The important story (from the standpoint of creativity theory) would begin at the representational level, and it would be at the representational level at which it would be most productive to pitch theories of creativity.

This has been the implicit assumption of all the creativity theories discussed thus far. Cognitive psychology has stressed the importance of representations, of symbol processing, and of explicit (although sometimes inexpressible) rules governing cognition. Until the advent of connectionism, the only challenge to the symbol-processing approach of cognitive psychology came from behaviorism, the theory that information processing supplanted as the principal paradigm of psychology.

In a sense, connectionism represents a resurrection of a central claim of behaviorism in the two theories' shared rejection of implied but unobservable cognitive "states"—internal representations of meaning, intentions, desires, and the like—as causal agents in cognition and behavior. Minsky (1986) argued that "what we call 'consciousness' consists of little more than menu lists that flash, from time to time, on mental screen displays" (p. 49) and that "consciousness does not concern the present, but the past; it has to do with how we think about the records of our recent thoughts" (p. 151). Similarly, it may be that divergent thinking, associations among concepts, and all other hypothesized creative-thinking processes are not actually actors in the cognitive drama, but merely incidental artifacts, created by psychologists to help them categorize their observations. These conceptual artifacts may play no causal role whatsoever in creative thought and performance. Just as Minsky would have us believe that consciousness is simply our way of trying to understand thought processes to which we have no direct access, divergent thinking and other purported creative-thinking skills and mechanisms may simply be ways for us to try to make sense of processes that actually operate at a much lower, nonrepresentational level.

It must be stressed that the argument from a strong connectionist perspective is not that connectionist networks lead in some way to divergent-thinking or other higher level creative-thinking skills, which in turn operate (perhaps together with other higher level skills) on conceptual representations of some kind, with the end result of creative thinking or performance. Eliminative connectionism argues that the higher level layers of divergent-thinking and other creative thinking skills play no role whatsoever in creative thought or performance. Appeal to such higher level skills may be a convenient way to summarize our observations of creative thinking, but if the eliminative connectionist story is the true one, such skills have no more influence on creative thinking than a "Monday morning quarterback" has on the previous Sunday afternoon's game.

Strong and weak connectionism, as described earlier, represent extreme scenarios. There are many points midway between the two, such as the position of Miikkulainen and Dyer (1991), who took a connectionist approach to natural language processing:

> Higher level tasks usually require composite subtasks. ... Complex behavior requires bringing together several different kinds of knowledge and processing, which is not possible without structure. ... A plausible approach for higher level cognitive modeling, therefore, is to construct the architecture from several interacting modules, which work together to produce the higher level behavior. (p. 344)

This is very similar to the approach favored by Minsky (1986), who noted that "any brain, machine, or other thing that has a mind must be composed of smaller things that cannot think at all" (p. 322).

Middle-ground connectionist theories argue that, at some level, discrete symbolic processors emerge from a connectionist substrate. At that level, these processors interact in an information-processing mode. This is similar to a weak connectionist scenario, because a connectionist architecture is acting as the foundation from which an information-processing system is built. The difference is that there may be important connectionist layers of cognition that are opaque from a representational point of view. But the important questions are the same here as in any information-processing system:

1. At what level or levels do symbolic processors emerge?
2. Do low-level symbolic processors join together to form higher level, general-purpose processors?

These two questions boil down to a single key question: What are the important cognitive-processing mechanisms? There are many possibilities regarding creative-thinking skills. It may be, for instance, that some very general cognitive skills, although identifiable through observation, are actually just convenient ways of classifying cognitive behavior that have no actual influence on cognition at all, as eliminative connectionism insists; and yet, although such high-level skills may not play a causal role in cognition, there may nonetheless be intermediate-level cognitive skills operating on a representational, rule-governed level. For example, it is possible that, although there is no general skill of divergent thinking (or of fluency, flexibility, etc.), there may nonetheless be a skill of divergent-thinking in some limited domain (e.g., the domains described by Gardner's, 1983, verbal, mathematical-logical, and other "intelligences"). It is also possible that the highest level of skill that takes an active part in creative thinking is much lower still, at the level, perhaps, of almost single-task-specific skills such as "thinking of words that rhyme with a given sound" or "thinking of unusual ways to group geometric shapes."

There is, then, no connectionist theory of creativity per se. If eliminative connectionism is correct, then that theory is the only basic-level theory needed to explain all of cognition, and any separate theory of creativity becomes superfluous.

Even if a somewhat weaker version of connectionism tells the true story, however, a connectionist approach to creativity is still a powerful reminder that we must be careful about the levels at which we think about creativity and construct our theories to explain it. The pre-representational level of the important elements in connectionist models, in which there is no way to describe the elements because they have no meaning apart from their place in the system as a whole, should at the very least remind us that more than one kind or level of analysis is often needed by psychological theories.

The importance of multiple levels of analysis suggested by the foregoing discussion of a connectionist approach may be significant even if connectionism's worst-case scenario is true and all levels of interest are representational and rule governed (and therefore amenable to description in terms of meaningful elements and their relationships). It is argued in chapter 6 that in the case of creativity, both causal, explanatory theories and descriptive, noncausal theories—operating at different levels—may be appropriate. It is also proposed that even when a higher level descriptive theory is formulated in terms of skills or mechanisms that actually have no causal effect whatsoever, such a descriptive theory may nonetheless show psychologists where to look for causal, explanatory theories of creative performance.

# 3

# Empirical Evidence for the Divergent-Thinking Theory of Creativity

The divergent-thinking theory of creativity has a great deal of intuitive appeal, especially the suggestion that creativity will be enhanced by considering, in the process of looking for new ideas or designing a solution to a problem, all of the following: (a) many, as opposed to only a few, ideas; (b) a wide range of ideas; and (c) unusual (as well as more typical) ideas. If not quite commonsensical, these strategies are at least not surprising, and it is hard to imagine seriously arguing that they would not, in general, result in more creative ideas and solutions to problems.

This is not only because divergent thinking has become almost synonymous with creativity. It is true, of course, that the general acceptance of divergent thinking as a kind of shorthand for creativity has probably colored the way our society (and its psychologists) think about creativity. This belief that creativity is rooted in divergent thinking may have subtle effects; for example, it may influence the outcome of experiments in which raters are asked to rate individuals globally for creativity. When other frames of reference are available (as, e.g., in an experiment in which experts in a field are asked to rate products in that field for creativity), the implicit equating of creativity with divergent thinking would reasonably be expected to have less influence on raters' judgments. But in an ill-defined situation such as global ratings of individuals for creativity, the commonly held belief that creativity and divergent thinking are related might exert considerable influence.

There is more to the appeal of these ideas than indoctrination by a generation of divergent-thinking testing and theorizing, however; there is, it can be argued, a certain almost irrefutable logic to them. As early as the 17th century, a similar idea was being argued (in a 1645 pamphlet on liberty of conscience):

> I know there is but one truth, but this truth cannot be so easily brought forth without this liberty; and a general restraint, though intended but for errors, yet through the unskillfulness of men, may fall upon the truth. And better many errors of some kind suffered than one useful truth be obstructed or destroyed. (quoted by Boorstin, 1958, pp. 8–9)

This sounds strangely familiar, almost like a late 20th-century creativity trainer exhorting trainees to "defer judgment," reminding them that "it takes at least a dozen bad ideas to produce one good idea," or encouraging them to "go for a large quantity of ideas first, and wait to judge the quality of those ideas later."

This is good advice, certainly, at least to a degree. But divergent-thinking theory does not say how long one should defer judgment, or how much time should be spent in idea generation prior to choosing a solution. It might be, as Howard Gruber has suggested, that a little divergent thinking is all that is needed—"just the idea that you shouldn't fall too deeply in love with your first effort" (H. E. Gruber, personal communication, September 18, 1991). One might not need to be a talented divergent thinker to be creative—in fact, it is possible that too much divergent thinking could be as much of an obstacle to creative thinking as too little!

One can therefore believe that deferring judgment, considering more than the first idea that springs to mind, and seeking unusual ideas can all be helpful strategies for improving creative thinking without endorsing the divergent-thinking theory of creativity. Divergent-thinking theory does not predict that a small or moderate amount of divergent thinking is optimal: According to standard divergent-thinking theories (and all the variants of these common divergent-thinking theories of which I am aware), any increase in divergent-thinking skill should lead, other things being equal, to some increase in creative performance. Even if a divergent-thinking theory proposed, as it might be reasonable to argue, that there would typically be "diminishing returns" in the value of each additional increase in divergent-thinking activity or skill (in keeping with the current interest in economic models of creativity; see, e.g., Rubenson & Runco, in press; Runco, 1991a; Sternberg & Lubart, 1991), this would not put a limit on how much divergent thinking would be helpful. It would, however, at least acknowledge that after a certain amount of divergent-thinking activity (or degree of divergent-thinking skill), further increases would lead to only very modest increases in creative performance.

Divergent-thinking theory, as it will be considered later, is thus committed to a "more is better" understanding of the role of divergent thinking in creativity, even if the relationship between divergent-thinking skill or activity and creativity is not a directly linear one. As such, measures of divergent thinking and of creative performance should, according to divergent-thinking theory, be highly correlated.

The research reported in chapters 4 and 5 calls into question the validity of all common divergent-thinking theories of creativity (which I consider as a single theory, using the theory embodied in the Torrance Tests of Creativity as the standard theory). Because a great deal of research has been conducted under the umbrella of this theoretical paradigm, a challenge to this paradigm is reasonable only if it is possible either to reinterpret or to find flaws in the body of research that claims to support the divergent-thinking theory of creativity. A review of the research that supports the predictive validity of the divergent-thinking theory is therefore presented in the first part of this chapter, followed by a review of research into the effects of divergent-thinking training on creativity. These reviews are not exhaustive, but by providing an overview of some of the most frequently cited studies, they demonstrate the problems and limitations of previous research designed to assess (a) the validity of the standard divergent-thinking model, and (b) the general effects of creativity training that is based on divergent-thinking theory.

## PREDICTIVE VALIDITY OF DIVERGENT-THINKING TEST SCORES

Torrance (1972b, 1990) reported 12 studies by several researchers of short-term predictive validity of the Torrance tests involving kindergarten through adult subjects, with sample sizes ranging from 12 to 133. The predicted creative behaviors in these studies include psychiatrists' assessments (via projective techniques) of fourth-grade students' sense of humor and strength of self-image, originality of stories written by sixth-grade students, a measure of the Piagetian concept of conservation among kindergarten and first-grade students, and teaching success in inner-city schools.

As valuable as some of these criterion variables are in and of themselves, little justification is given for identifying them with creativity. Torrance (1972b) acknowledged that some studies conducted by other investigators have resulted in zero or negative correlations between divergent-thinking scores and criterion variables such as course grades and classroom misbehavior. He dismissed these as "irrelevant," as there is "no logical reason to expect scores on the Torrance Test of Creative Thinking to be related to such measures" (p. 242).

Unfortunately, a similar complaint might be lodged against many of the criterion variables that have shown significant correlations with Torrance test scores. As a group, these studies neither support nor discredit the divergent-thinking theory of creativity because the criterion variables utilized are not clearly related to creative performance.

Torrance (1972a, 1972b, 1990) also reported the results of six long-term correlational studies of the predictive validity of his tests, and it is on the basis of these studies that he made his strongest claim for the validity of the Torrance tests. Two of these he has termed *major* studies (Torrance, 1972b, p. 245, 1990, p. 6) because they involved more subjects, longer time periods, and more rigorous procedures. The following analysis considers only one of these studies, the major study employing the largest number of subjects and the one Torrance (1990) cited first in his most recent publication about the validity of his tests. The results of the other studies—especially the other major study—tend to be similar. The problems in interpreting the results of this largest and most comprehensive study, which are discussed here, also apply in a general way to the other long-term studies.

In 1959, all 392 students at the University of Minnesota High School (Grades 7–12) were given the Torrance Tests of Creative Thinking. This was a highly able group, with a mean IQ of 118 and a mean national-norm percentile rank on the Iowa Tests of Educational Development of 84.

In the most important follow-up study of these students 12 years later, 236 of the ex-students completed questionnaires. There were three key indices drawn from the subjects' responses:

1. Quantity of Creative Achievements: This included reports of subscribing to a professional journal; learning a new language; writing songs, plays, poems, or stories; changing religious affiliation; receiving research grants; performing on television or radio; handling in-service education for co-workers; publishing a scientific paper; and giving a public music recital.

2. Quality of Creative Achievements: Respondents were asked to write about their three most creative achievements. These were scored on a 10-point scale for creativity by independent judges.

3. Creativity of Aspirations: Respondents were asked to write about what they would like to do in the future. These future aspirations were evaluated for creativity on a 10-point scale by independent judges.

The results were consistently positive. Correlations of the three criterion variables with subscale scores of the Torrance test taken 12 years previously ranged from .27 to .45, all of which were significant at the .01 level.

Interpretation of these results is problematic, however. They can be questioned on at least three grounds: (a) relevance of the criterion variables to creativity, (b) multi-collinearity among measures of divergent thinking and measures of intelligence, and (c) similarity in form of the Torrance test and the follow-up questionnaires.

As with the short-term studies, the criterion variables used in this long-term study are questionable as measures of creativity. This is especially true of the Quantity of Creative Achievement measure. These activities are all accomplishments (although of varying degrees), but it is difficult to assess, based on self-report, how creative these accomplishments might be. As Crockenberg (1972) noted, "given the creativity criteria used ... [the results] should not be taken too seriously" (p. 35).

All of the criterion variables are the kinds of things one might predict of intelligent people, and the correlations Torrance (1972b) reported between intelligence and the three criterion variables are in the same range as the correlations between the divergent-thinking test scores and the criterion variables. Torrance test scores, in turn, are significantly correlated with intelligence test scores (Wallach, 1970). Unfortunately, as Kogan (1983) pointed out:

Torrance and his associates appear reluctant to make use of multiple-regression analyses that would yield information about the incremental validity of the Torrance instruments over and beyond the predictive power of IQ. ... Until such analyses are carried out, evidence for long-term predictive validity of the Torrance instruments must be considered equivocal at best. (p. 650)

A final criticism of Torrance's (1972a, 1972b, 1990) 12-year study involves the similarity in form and scoring of the Torrance test and the criterion variables. The Torrance Verbal test was used in this study. (There is also a figural test, in which subjects respond to most prompts with drawings rather than words.) Responses to questions like listing as many "interesting and unusual uses" (Torrance, 1966, p.

10) of cardboard boxes as possible were scored for fluency, flexibility, originality, and elaboration, with fluency—the number of different responses—accounting for most of the total score variance, as noted earlier (Heausler & Thompson, 1988; Kogan, 1983). There is a premium on quantity, and the more one writes, the higher one's divergent-thinking score will generally be. This was also true of at least one of the criterion variables used in this study (Quantity of Creative Achievements), and because all three variables involved writing answers to be judged on the basis of either quantity or quality, it is possible that the shared variance on all three criterion measures and Torrance test scores reflects writing ability in tasks such as these, not real-world creative accomplishment. The Torrance Verbal test and the Quantity of Creative Achievements, Quality of Creative Achievements, and Creativity of Aspirations questionnaires may therefore all be measures of skill at a particular kind of writing task—or perhaps they are all indices of creativity on this kind of writing task—and yet be of little nor no value in predicting other kinds of creative performance.

Studies conducted using other measures of divergent thinking than the Torrance tests have not done much to support the divergent-thinking theory of creativity. Cropley (1972) administered a battery of Guilford-type divergent-production tests to junior high school subjects and assessed achievement in four nonacademic areas (art, drama, literature, and music) 5 years later. Although Cropley initially reported significant correlations, a re-analysis by Jordan (1975) pointed out that Cropley's results were erroneous, and in fact there were no significant correlations at all.

Kogan and Pankove (1974) used the Wallach and Kogan (1965a) divergent-thinking tasks in a study that tested students in the 5th and 10th grades, and then gave them a questionnaire about their activities and accomplishments when they were high school seniors. The fifth-grade divergent-thinking scores did not predict overall accomplishments as reported 7 years later. Tenth-grade divergent-thinking test scores "made a marginally significant contribution" (Kogan & Pankove, 1974, p. 802) in predicting activities and accomplishments 2 years later. Intellective-aptitude measures from Grades 5 and 10, however, accounted for "modest to substantial" (p. 802) amounts of variance in 12th-grade activities and accomplishments, greater at both grade levels than the amount of variance accounted for by 5th- and 10th-grade divergent-thinking test scores.

The Kogan and Pankove (1974) study is similar to the Torrance (1972a, 1972b, 1990) long-term study reported earlier, and the failure to replicate the results may be due to an important difference in the tests. The Torrance test is significantly correlated with intelligence, but the Wallach and Kogan test is not (Crockenberg, 1972; Kogan, 1983; Wallach, 1970). The lack of predictive power of the Wallach and Kogan test thus supports the interpretation that Torrance's result may be due to a multi-collinearity problem, under which divergent thinking adds no additional predictive power beyond that of measured IQ.

Although he found only limited multi-collinearity between measures of intelligence and ideational fluency, Hocevar (1980) reported that neither kind of test was able to predict creativity with more than modest accuracy, and that there were great differences in predictive ability of the two different kinds of measures across domains. Hocevar used a self-report inventory of creative activities and achievements as his index of creativity. After demonstrating in a study of 94 university students the limited ability of divergent-thinking indices to predict creativity—and the equal, and in some cases superior, ability of a traditional intelligence test to make such predictions—Hocevar noted that it is ironic that divergent-thinking tests are not better able to predict creativity than simple measures of intelligence, given the long history of criticism of intelligence tests for not predicting creativity.

Anastasi (1982), in a discussion of divergent-thinking tests of creativity, concluded that "evidence of relation between the Torrance Tests and everyday-life criteria of creative achievement is meager" (p. 391). Anastasi also noted that a major factor analytic study of the performance of 800 fifth-grade students (Yamamoto & Frengel, 1966) provided no support for a single-factor interpretation. The factors identified in this study were highly task specific.

Runco (1986c, 1990) suggested the need to consider the domain-specificity of creativity when analyzing the ability of divergent-thinking measures to predict creative performance. It is possible, under this interpretation, that divergent-thinking skills are important in creative performance, but that each of these skills is relevant only to one of many specific performance domains (such as Gardner's, 1983, "intelligences," as Runco, 1990, suggested) or to even more narrowly defined tasks within those domains.

It seems fair to conclude, as Kogan (1983) and Crockenberg (1972) did in their review articles, that the predictive validity of divergent-thinking tests has not been established. It is not clear that such validation is impossible, either by more carefully controlled studies with the Torrance tests (which seem the most likely candidates among existing tests) or with some future divergent-thinking test. In the meantime, the divergent-thinking theory maintains its grip on creativity testing, theory, and training. In the next section, the results of training in divergent thinking are examined to see what support can be garnered for a divergent-thinking theory of creativity.

## EVALUATIONS OF THE EFFECTS OF TRAINING IN DIVERGENT THINKING

Creativity-training programs provide a unique research opportunity to test theories of creativity. If a training program based on a particular theory of creativity can demonstrate that it improves creative performance, this success can also count as evidence in favor of the theory. Conversely, failure of such a training program to improve creative performance can count as evidence against the theory on which it is based. Successes and failures of creativity-training programs allow multiple interpretations, of course: The effects of any such program may derive from factors involved in training unrelated to the theory upon which the training is nominally based. The design of evaluation studies is therefore both critically important and exceedingly difficult.

Creativity-training programs also allow research into ways that creative-thinking skills, strategies, and procedures might be different for subjects who have had training and those who have not. It may be, as suggested in the revised theory of divergent thinking described in chapter 2, that those who have been trained in some skill such as divergent thinking will show different patterns of linkage between divergent-thinking skills and creative behavior than those without such training. It is with these two goals in mind—(a) assessing the theoretical significance of the results of creativity-training studies, and (b) inquiring into what they suggest about how the patterns of creative performance of trained and untrained subjects on tests of creativity and divergent-thinking skill might differ—that past research into the effects of creativity training is examined here.

There are a variety of creativity-training programs, most of which include divergent thinking as a major component (e.g., Baer, 1988b; Covington, Crutchfield, Davies, & Olton, 1974; Crabbe, 1985; Feldhusen, Treffinger, & Bahlke, 1970; Gordon, 1961; Gourley, 1981; Hoomes, 1986; Isaksen & Parnes, 1985; Mayer, 1983, 1987; Micklus & Micklus, 1986; Myers & Torrance, 1964; National Talent Network, 1989; Olton & Crutchfield, 1969; Osborn, 1963; Parnes, 1972, 1985; Parnes & Noller, 1973, 1974; Perkins, 1981; Rose & Lin, 1984; Rubinstein, 1975, 1980; von Oech, 1983). These programs make diverse claims for their success in promoting creative thinking. If such claims could be substantiated, they would appear to support the divergent-thinking theory of creativity and to contradict the claim that general creative-thinking skills like divergent thinking do not play a significant role in creative performance.

There are at least two explanations of how creativity might be enhanced by training in divergent thinking that do not contradict the evidence (presented in chapter 4) that no general creative-thinking skill is a significant contributor to creative performance in untrained subjects. It is possible, as noted in chapter 2, that divergent thinking may play a role in the creativity only of those trained in divergent thinking. It is also possible that something other than training in divergent thinking might account for the success of such programs, such as training in task-specific skills relevant to the particular tasks used to measure creativity (as suggested by Mansfield, Busse, & Krepelka, 1978, and Mayer, 1983).

Rose and Lin (1984) did a comprehensive meta-analysis of the long-term effects of creativity-training programs. Unfortunately (for the purposes of testing the divergent-thinking theory of creativity), Rose and Lin included only studies that used the Torrance tests as the primary outcome measure. Their analysis showed that the 46 programs they included in their study were, in general, quite successful: the average overall effect size was .468. Looking only at the group of programs that had the most consistent effect—the Osborn-Parnes Creative Problem Solving (CPS) program (Parnes, 1972; Parnes & Noller, 1973, 1974)— an average effect size of .629 was found for the eight studies in which this training program was used.

These results suggest that creativity-training programs that emphasize divergent thinking can lead to substantial increases in scores on the Torrance Tests of Creative Thinking (especially the verbal tests, which showed significantly larger increases after training than the figural tests). This is not evidence for the validity of the divergent-thinking theory of creativity, however. What has been demonstrated is that training in divergent thinking improves divergent-thinking test scores. Unfortunately, until a connection between divergent thinking and creativity can be demonstrated, these studies provide no evidence as to whether the creativity of trainees in these programs has been affected in any way.

There have been evaluations of creativity-training programs that have not relied on Torrance tests or other tests of divergent thinking (e.g., Baer, 1988b; Mansfield, Busse, & Krepelka, 1978; Olton & Crutchfield, 1969). The results have been mixed, and the programs that have been most successful have been criticized for claiming to improve general creative-thinking ability based on test results that show only that students improved in the specific kind of problem solving taught in the course (Mayer, 1983; Mansfield, Busse, & Krepelka, 1978). Furthermore, none of these programs teaches divergent thinking exclusively, but only as one component in multi-step processes. Thus even if clear gains in creative performance were demonstrated, it would be impossible to separate the gains attributable to divergent-thinking training from those due to other components in the program.

## SUMMARY AND OUTLINE OF THE ARGUMENT THAT FOLLOWS

In summary, evaluations of creativity-training programs that emphasize divergent thinking have been shown to result in substantial increases in divergent-thinking test scores. These training programs have not been shown to increase creativity, however. This remains an unresolved—and essentially untested—empirical question, because the designs of all studies conducted thus far do not allow us to draw any conclusions on this issue. If one accepts the conclusion of the previous section—that the predictive validity of divergent-thinking test scores for creativity is unproven—then evaluations of creativity-training programs do not provide evidence to support the divergent-thinking theory of creativity. Neither, it should be added, do they provide evidence against this theory. The contribution of divergent thinking to creative performance thus remains an undemonstrated (although widely accepted) hypothesis.

The major purpose of the two studies reported in chapter 5 was to determine whether training in divergent thinking enhances creativity across a variety of performance domains. As is shown in that chapter, significant evidence that divergent-thinking training can improve creative performance on a variety of tasks was indeed found, presenting an interesting problem of interpretation.

Despite the evidence (reviewed in detail in chapter 4) against the existence of general creative-thinking skills, there is at least one explanation of the effects claimed for training in divergent thinking on creative performance that would still allow for a significant role to be played by divergent thinking, although only among trained subjects. The revised divergent-thinking theory of creativity (described in chapter 2) could account for both the absence of evidence for any significant effects of divergent thinking on the creative performance of untrained subjects and the presence of evidence for significant effects of divergent-thinking training on creative performance.

The research reported in chapter 5 was, for these reasons, designed to gather evidence (a) to determine whether training in divergent thinking does indeed enhance creative performance in a variety of task domains, and, if such effects are demonstrated (as they were), (b) to provide evidence on which to base a choice among two competing explanations of those effects. Those two explanations of what might cause such effects are:

1. A revised divergent-thinking theory of creativity, an interpretation that allows a significant role for a general, domain-transcending thinking skill in creative performance among subjects trained in when to apply divergent-thinking skills, and
2. Training in task-specific skills incidental to divergent-thinking training.

Either interpretation would be consistent with research results (presented in chapter 4) that deny the importance of general, domain-transcending thinking skills (such as divergent thinking) in the creative performance of subjects untrained in divergent thinking.

# 4

# Research on the Generality of Creative Performance Across Domains*

As noted in chapter 1, there is a strong attraction among scientists to general, domain-transcending theories, and this attraction is equally true no matter what the topic under investigation. General theories, if true, can explain much more than domain-specific theories, and they provide a simpler and more unified understanding of a range of phenomena. Theories of creativity, theories of intelligence, and theories of the forces of nature, for example, would all be more powerful if those theories could be all-inclusive, rather than limited in their application to narrow domains. General theories also allow results of research involving tasks or materials characteristic of one domain to be applied readily to the activities of other domains.

This is how we would like our theories to operate, as grand unifying visions that allow us to see, with a single lens, the broadest possible landscape of phenomena in the greatest possible detail. But even the most general theory has its limits: A grand unifying theory in physics, for example, would not have much to say about why birds build nests, or why some people write more creative poems than others. And so the question we need to ask of a theory is not whether it includes everything, but rather how much it can profitably include—and, conversely, what are its limits.

In the field of creativity, many researchers, theorists, and trainers have thought of creativity as a general intellectual trait that will affect a person's performance regardless of the particular activity in which they happen to be engaged (Draper, 1985; Hennessey & Amabile, 1988a; Simon, 1967; Tardif & Sternberg, 1988; Torrance & Presbury, 1984; Treffinger, 1986). Domain-relevant skills and knowledge have also been acknowledged to be important contributors to creative

---

*Many of the results of Studies 1–4 were previously reported in the *Journal of Creative Behavior* (Baer, 1991), although in somewhat less detail. Study 5 was incomplete at that time, but some preliminary results of Study 5 were also reported in the same *Journal of Creative Behavior* article.

With the exception of Study 5, which was conducted as a part of regular classroom writing activities by the professor of an English composition class, all creativity testing in Studies 1–4 and 6–7 (reported in chapter 5) was conducted by the author.

mance (Amabile, 1983; Gruber & Davis, 1988; Tardif & Sternberg, 1988; Weisberg, 1988), and the importance of such skills is difficult to deny. For example, the ability to read music and play an instrument would probably help a composer produce more creative scores, but would be of little value to a landscape artist; whereas skill in sketching, knowledge of how to stretch a canvas, and training in the use of perspective would be likely to help a painter produce more creative landscapes, but would probably have little impact on the creative output of a composer. But even among those who have discussed the importance of domain-relevant skills and knowledge, this is typically only one part of a larger picture. Creativity has been viewed as something that goes beyond domain-dependent knowledge and skill, in both conventional wisdom and most creativity theories.

Creativity as a general skill or trait has been defined in many ways: as habits of thought, attitudes, personality traits, or skill in the use of problem-solving heuristics (Darley, Glucksberg, & Kinchla, 1986). What all such definitions have in common is that they transcend performance domains. It is this monolithic view of creativity, in which some skill or attribute is believed to influence creative performance regardless of the task domain, that has guided most research in creativity (Tardif & Sternberg, 1988; Torrance & Presbury, 1984).

The most influential of these general creativity-relevant factors or theories has been the theory of divergent thinking. As discussed in chapters 2 and 3, it is typically assumed, either explicitly or implicitly, that divergent-thinking skills are easily transferable from one task to another—that they transcend the particular task on which they are observed or measured, and can therefore contribute to creative performance in all (or at least many) task domains. Any challenge to the generality of creativity across performance domains is therefore a challenge to the divergent-thinking theory of creativity, as well to as to all other theories that posit the existence of such general creativity-relevant traits or skills.

Just as general, all-encompassing theories have in the past decade been called into question in many other fields (see chapter 1), so the common assumption that creativity is a general cognitive trait or set of traits that underlie creative performance in diverse domains has also recently been challenged. For example, Langley and Jones (1988), as a result of their studies of scientific creativity, argued that "humans possess no general creativity factor" (p. 199).

This is in marked contrast to an assertion made by Langley in his earlier work (Langley, Simon, Bradshaw, & Zytkow, 1987) that the work of discovery is in all cases an exercise in normal problem solving shared by "all forms of serious human thought—in science, in the arts, in the professions, in school, in personal life" (p. 6). This quote echoes the writing of the article's second author, Simon, who wrote two decades earlier:

> that the creative process in art and in science are substantially identical, that however much the "two cultures" may be divided in our society—however little scientists may know about the arts or artists about science—the processes they use in their respective fields when they are being creative are basically the same kinds of thinking processes. (Simon, 1967, p. 44)

Langley and Jones, in their 1988 article, appear to have moved far from Simon's single-process position to a more contextual, task-specific view of creative thinking. They argued for a model of creativity that is related more closely to "spreading activation" mechanisms of memory processes than to heuristic-based, "problem space" search processes.

In studies of a very different sort, Runco (1986b, 1987) and Hocevar (1976, 1978) used self-report questionnaires to assess the generality of creativity in individuals. Hocevar reported a high degree of generality in the self-reported creative performance of college students, but Runco argued that this effect is somewhat an artifact of the method used to collect information. The generality that Hocevar reported, according to Runco's analysis, is limited to the quantity of creative activity rather than the quality of creative activity. Runco used self-report techniques with fifth- through eighth-grade students and found low correlations among the quality of creative performances in different domains. His subjects reported higher correlations among the quantity of such activities in each domain than among the quality of those performances.

In a later study using performance evaluations by experts, Runco (1989) had artists rate three different art projects of 37 upper elementary students. In this study, Runco employed a consensual rating technique similar to the one used by Amabile (1982, 1983), and also similar to the approach used in Studies 1–7 reported later in this chapter and in chapter 5. Inter-item correlations ranged from -.10 to .29, indicating little generality of creative performance even within the domain of art. The projects themselves were diverse: one was a crayon drawing of a limerick, another a collage of a dragon, and the third a large picture decorated with colored pens, pencils, crayons, and tempura.

Writing about creativity in the arts, Winner (1982) argued that "any single theory designed to explain creativity as if it were one process, used alike by artists and scientists, is likely to be incomplete" (p. 49). She went beyond domain-specificity to hypothesize that there is no such thing as "the" creative process, even within a particular domain, because of the variability among the many artists in that domain, each using, for example, a different mixture of conscious craft and irrational, primary-process thought.

Tardif and Sternberg (1988), in summing up the views of recent creativity theorists, wrote that although "it is generally acknowledged that people are creative within particular domains of endeavor ... when the issue of domain specificity occurs in discussions of creative processes, much less agreement ensues" (p. 433). Of the writers that Tardif and Sternberg surveyed, the domain-transcending, one-factor-fits-all approach to understanding the creative process has been challenged most directly by Gardner (1983, 1988), who argued that "cognition ought to be decomposed into a number of parts, modules, or factors, with each operating according to its own set of principles" (1988, p. 300). This means, according to Gardner (1988), that we should "no longer speak (except in shorthand) of an individual as creative; instead, one would recognize the possibilities of creativity in specific domains" (pp. 300–301).

Gardner (1983) proposed that there are at least seven different "intelligences" (seven discrete domains of cognition), each operating according to its own set of rules and each representing a distinct kind of thinking and problem solving. The seven intelligences are linguistic, logical mathematical, spatial, bodily kinesthetic, interpersonal, and intrapersonal.

More recently, Gardner (1988) advocated the extension of these seven domains, and the modular view of intelligence that they represent, to our understanding of creative thinking. It was this view of creative thinking, in which the cognitive processes that underlie creative performance in various domains are shared within but not across domains, that motivated Study 1.

## GENERAL OVERVIEW OF THE RESEARCH DESIGN OF STUDIES 1–5

In the series of studies reported later, I examine the creative performance of individuals on several tasks, using multiple regression and correlational analyses to determine if the creative performance of individuals on one task is predictive of their creative performance on other tasks. If (a) general-purpose, domain-transcending creative-thinking processes (such as divergent thinking) make substantial contributions to creative performance on different tasks, and if (b) there are individual differences in these thinking skills, then individuals who are creative on one task should, on average and other things being equal, be creative on other tasks in different domains. Conversely, low creativity on one task should be predictive of low creativity on other tasks.

The principal goal of the research reported in this chapter has been to investigate the generality of creative-thinking skills across a variety of creativity-relevant tasks among subjects untrained in divergent-thinking skills. The evidence that the research reported in this chapter provides against the significance of any general, domain-transcending creative-thinking skills in subjects untrained in divergent-thinking techniques provides a key rationale for additional investigations (Studies 6 and 7, reported in chapter 5) into whether such general skills might play a role in the creative performance of subjects who have received such divergent-thinking training.

Research in creativity requires some kind of assessment procedure. This is an obstacle that has plagued the field (Amabile, 1983; Anderson, 1980; Mayer, 1983; Treffinger, 1986). The most commonly used measures of creativity, as noted earlier, have been the Torrance Tests of Creativity (Torrance, 1990; Torrance & Presbury, 1984). These tests assume the existence of general creative-thinking skills (specifically, divergent thinking) that transcend domain. They cannot, therefore, be used to test whether such skills in fact exist.

Performance measures of creativity mimic the way creativity is assessed in real-world domains. Torrance himself recommended the use of a wide variety of indicators of creativity (Torrance, 1984), and noted a trend in recent research with adults toward the use of more "real-life" measures (Torrance & Presbury, 1984). In studies using such performance measures, the creativity of works of art, sonnets, scientific theories, and other products is determined by a consensus of experts in the appropriate domains. Such consensus is achieved informally, of course, and the experts who contribute to it may or may not be able to state explicitly the criteria upon which they base their judgments (and when they do, they may disagree). Even in physics, where experimental "proofs" might seem to hold sway, creativity is not judged by some absolute standard. Scientific theories, like poems and paintings, are judged by a consensus of those deemed knowledgeable in the field (Kuhn, 1970). The standards (which are dictated by the currently dominant paradigm) may change over time, but at any given time, the best assessment—in fact, the only meaningful assessment—of the creativity of a product is the collective opinion of those considered experts in that domain.

It should be noted that this is not the same as the evaluations used by Torrance (1972a, 1972b, 1990) in the long-term study described in chapter 2. The only "creative products" evaluated in those studies were subjects' responses to questionnaires. This is not the same as evaluating the creativity of the activities and products described in the questionnaire responses. Performance measures of creativity employ expert judges to assess the creativity of actual creative products, not subjects' descriptions of their activities.

Although they are time consuming to use and generally not suitable for situations requiring standardized scoring for large numbers of subjects tested at different times and places, performance measures of creativity may be the best measures of creativity available for many research purposes because of their similarity to actual creative productions. They also have the advantage of not confounding hypotheses about the nature of creativity (such as the thesis that creativity is a divergent-thinking skill, or any skill or set of skills that are domain independent) with the assessment of creative performance. Although relatively new as assessment procedures (Amabile, 1979, 1982, 1983; Amabile, Hennessey, & Grossman, 1986; Connecticut State Department of Education, 1988; Hennessey & Amabile, 1988a, 1988b; Gardner, 1989), such measures are closely related to the tasks that critics evaluate in determining real-world creative achievement, whether the domain is poetry, landscape gardening, science, or teaching. (It must be acknowledged that some domains avail themselves more readily to such tests, both in the laboratory and the real world. Poetry, e.g., offers poems for ready [albeit subjective] evaluation, whereas the appropriate products for the assessment of scientific creativity are less easily identified.)

The following studies utilized performance measures of creativity. In doing so, they were modeled on the work of Amabile and her colleagues (Amabile, 1979, 1982, 1983; Amabile, Hennessey, & Grossman, 1986; Hennessey & Amabile, 1988a, 1988b), who have used experts in a variety of domains to assess the creativity of products such as collages and poems, and who have demonstrated both the reliability and validity of the technique in more than 30 independent investigations (Hennessey & Amabile, 1988a). The technique relies on what Johnson-Laird (1988b) termed the "central paradox of creativity" (p. 208): people are typically better critics than they are creators. For most of us, "critical abilities are more advanced than productive abilities" (Perkins, 1981, p. 128), and we are able to judge the creativity of products that we ourselves could not create—and judge them with a high interjudge reliability (Amabile, 1982, 1983).

## Study 1: Eighth-Grade Students

Fifty eighth-grade students were given five creativity tests: (a) writing a poem, (b) writing a short story, (c) writing a mathematical word problem, (d) writing a mathematical equation, and (e) responding to a one-item verbal-fluency question. Only the verbal-fluency question was timed.

Tasks were selected from what are generally considered the verbal and mathematical domains because of the ready availability of related indices of skillful performance in these domains. Recent verbal IQ, mathematical IQ, reading achievement, and mathematical achievement test scores were obtained for all subjects. There is, of course, considerable multi-collinearity among these measures, with particularly high correlations between scores of verbal IQ and reading achievement and between scores of mathematical IQ and achievement in mathematics. Nonetheless, for both the verbal and mathematical domains, both IQ and achievement measures were used because they test somewhat different aspects of skillful performance, thus giving a broader picture of students' general ability to produce correct answers to domain-relevant questions.

There were two groups of 25 students (described later). Judges (described in Appendix B) with expertise in each task domain rank ordered the poems, stories, word problems, and equations for creativity. The verbal-fluency question was scored only for quantity of responses, rather than using multiple divergent-thinking subscales. As noted in chapter 2, scores obtained using only this easy-to-score and unambiguous measure of fluency correlate highly with divergent-thinking test scores based on more complex scoring procedures (Kogan, 1983).

Because the study was interested in factors leading to creative performance other than those that contribute to domain-specific skillful performance, the variance in the four primary creativity test scores attributable to domain-specific, skillful-performance factors was removed, and partial correlations among residual creativity test scores were computed.

The primary hypothesis of Study 1 was that creativity is not domain independent, and that creative performance in one domain should therefore not be predictive of creative performance in other domains. Specifically, it was predicted that residual creativity test scores (with variance shared by IQ and achievement tests removed) in poetry writing and story writing (two tasks falling within the linguistic domain) would not be correlated with residual creativity test scores in equation and word-problem creating (two tasks falling largely within the logical-mathematical domain).

A secondary hypothesis was that creative-thinking skills cluster in domains, and that these are the same domains (or intelligences) described by Gardner (1983). Creativity in one part of a domain should therefore be predictive of creativity in another part of the same domain. Specifically, it was predicted that creativity between the two verbal tasks (poetry writing and story writing) would be correlated, as would creativity between the two mathematics tasks (equation and word-problem creating).

A third hypothesis was that the single-item verbal-fluency test, which (because it is a test of a specific verbal skill) falls within the linguistic domain, would be correlated with the poetry- and story-writing creativity tests, but not with the two mathematical creativity tests.

## Method

### Subjects

Fifty eighth-grade students from two semi-rural middle schools in western Maryland served as subjects. There was one group of 25 students from each school; in both cases, the groups were composed of entire beginning algebra classes. Each group (by chance) contributed the same number of subjects and the same gender ratio: 15 females and 10 males. (There were actually 27 students in one of the classes, but because two students were absent the day of testing, they were not included in the study.) The subjects' verbal and mathematical IQ (Differential Abilities Test) and reading and mathematical achievement (California Achievement Test) test scores were well above average, as shown in Table 4.1. All standardized IQ and achievement testing took place within two months of the creativity testing as part of the two schools' regular testing programs.

### Tests

The single-item verbal-fluency test was the only timed test. Following a brief warm-up exercise (described later), subjects were given 3 minutes to list on paper all possible uses for discarded tin cans. This is a common format for divergent-thinking testing, and is in fact a variant of the "Unusual Uses" item of the Torrance Tests of Creative Thinking (Torrance, 1966) and somewhat similar to the format of Guilford's Alternate Uses Test (Christensen, Guilford, Merrifield, & Wilson, 1978), although the Guilford test allows only six responses and is scored for flexibility rather than fluency. This brief verbal-fluency test was scored simply by counting the number of different responses.

TABLE 4.1
Standardized Test Scores (Study 1)

| Test | Mean | Standard Deviation | Range |
|------|------|--------------------|-------|
| Verbal IQ[a] | 78.90 | 18.82 | 20–99 |
| Reading achievement[b] | 88.80 | 11.54 | 56–99 |
| Math IQ[a] | 85.18 | 12.91 | 50–99 |
| Math achievement[b] | 92.48 | 6.43 | 71–99 |

*Note.* All scores are reported as percentiles. Subjects were 30 females and 20 males, all eighth-grade students ages 12–14 years old.

[a]Differential Aptitude Test.

[b]California Achievement Test.

The other four tests (described here) were not timed. Most students finished all five tasks in about 2 hours, and all subjects finished in less than 3 hours.

*Poetry-Writing Test.* Subjects were asked to write an original poem on the topic of the four seasons. The form, style, and length of the poem were not specified. Subjects were told that, except for the topic, everything else about the poem was up to them.

*Story-Writing Test.* Subjects were given a drawing depicting two men, one neatly and one casually dressed, approaching the corner of a building from opposite directions. They were asked to write an original story in which the two men played some part.

*Word-Problem-Creating Test.* Subjects were asked to write an interesting and original math word problem. They were not asked to solve the problem, but instructed to make sure all needed information was included so that the problem could be solved by someone else.

*Equation-Creating Test.* Subjects were given examples of a few equalities (e.g., $2 + 2 = 2 + 2$; $[9/3][2/6] = [2/3][9/6]$) and asked to write an interesting, original equation.

Students' responses to these four creativity tests were typed and photocopied by the experimenter and then rank ordered for creativity by five qualified experts, who were paid for their work. The expertise of the judges depended on the test. For example, the poems were rated by poets and English teachers, and the equations were judged by mathematics teachers and mathematics professors.

In all cases, there was some mixture of backgrounds among the judges for a particular test. That is, in no case did all five have exactly the same job. However, each was an expert in the domain being judged, and in some cases (as in that of the mathematics teachers and mathematics professors who rated the equations), the difference between roles was more a relative difference rather than a categorical one. This heterogeneity among judges within domains was planned to help avoid introducing the bias of a single perspective (and the falsely high interrater reliability coefficients that such a systematic bias might engender). The heterogeneity among judges *across* domains was, of course, required to ensure expertise among the judges, as well as to avoid possible artifacts in ratings resulting from cross-domain stylistic preferences of the judges.

The judges were in all cases ignorant of the goal of the study and did not know the subjects of the study. The judges knew that their work was part of a study of creativity, but they were not aware of the hypotheses guiding the research. The instructions given to the students were explained to the judges fully, and they were informed that the subjects were all eighth-grade students. The definition of creativity used in judging the various products was expressly left up to each individual judge. Appendix A includes the actual instructions given to the judges, and Appendix B provides a description of the judges.

Each group of 25 papers was ranked for creativity by each judge from 1 to 25, and these rank-ordered scores were then converted using an area-under-the-curve table into normally distributed standard scores. This conversion was based on the assumption of a normal distribution of creativity in each of the groups of students. (Recalculations using original rank-ordered scores rather than converted scores yielded almost identical results, however, in this study and the two that followed it. In Studies 4 and 5, therefore, this somewhat cumbersome area-under-the-curve procedure was discontinued, as explained later.) Interrater reliabilities (computed using coefficient alpha) were in all cases high, ranging from .78 to .92 (see Table 4.2).

Each student's score on each test was the sum of the scores of the five judges for that paper.

### Procedure

All subjects were tested in their regular classrooms, although their regular class schedules were changed so that they would stay in the same classroom all morning (in one case) or all afternoon (in the other). Subjects were told that the experimenter was interested in the creative thinking of students like themselves, and that the activities they were going to do would help him understand this better. All were cooperative and appeared to work diligently on all tasks.

The verbal-fluency test was administered first in both cases. A warm-up verbal-fluency question was posed to the class by the experimenter ("How might you use old socks?"), and subjects were encouraged to contribute answers by raising their hands and sharing their ideas with the class. The experimenter stated that any and all responses were acceptable in this activity. He acknowledged each response and repeated it if it seemed likely that some students may not have heard it, but he did not comment (either favorably or unfavorably) on any of the responses given by students. This warm-up exercise was immediately followed by the timed verbal-fluency test.

The other tests were administered in reverse order in the two classes. (The order was poem/story/word problem/equation in one class and equation/word problem/story/poem in the other.) To avoid confusing the subjects by giving them too many instructions at the same time, the four tasks were not all described at once. The first task was introduced, and, after a period of time, subjects were interrupted

TABLE 4.2
Interrater Reliabilities (Study 1)

| Test | Reliability Coefficient[a] |
| --- | --- |
| Poetry | .86 |
| Story | .89 |
| Word problem | .78 |
| Equation | .92 |

*Note.* There were five judges for each test.
[a]Coefficient alpha (Nunnally, 1978).

to be told of the next task, with a new task introduced in this way approximately every 20 minutes. The subjects were told that they could work on each task as long as they wished, and that they could go back to previous tasks as often as they wished. Students who completed all tasks were free to do other work or to read silently at their desks.

## Results

Table 4.3 lists all zero-order correlations among creativity test scores and standardized IQ and achievement test scores.

Among the four creativity tests, the only significant correlations were between poetry writing and word-problem creating ($r = .31$, $p < .05$) and story writing and verbal fluency ($r = .34$, $p < .05$). As anticipated, verbal skill (as measured by the verbal IQ and reading achievement tests) contributed to creativity in verbal-domain tasks, and mathematical skill (as measured by the mathematical IQ and mathematical achievement tests) contributed to creativity in mathematical-domain tasks. There was considerable overlap on the word-problem-creating test, which involves both mathematical and verbal skills. In fact, scores on the word-problem-creating test were significantly correlated with three of the standardized tests—verbal IQ ($r = .38$, $p < .01$), reading comprehension ($r = .36$, $p < .01$), and mathematical IQ ($r = .51$, $p < .01$)—and the correlation between word-problem creating and mathematical achievement ($r = .26$) narrowly missed the .05 cut-off ($p < .07$).

As expected, the four standardized tests (verbal IQ, reading achievement, mathematical IQ, and mathematical achievement) were highly correlated with one another, with correlation coefficients ranging from .32 (mathematical IQ–reading achievement, $p < .01$) to .60 (verbal IQ–reading achievement, $p < .01$). Because the correlations among the creativity tests in Table 4.3 are confounded by this expected multi-collinearity problem, this examination of zero-order correlation coefficients was not the primary planned analysis of the results. A more clear (although not radically different) picture emerges when the variance shared by each of the creativity tests and the four standardized tests is removed from the creativity tests' variance and the partial correlations among the residual scores are examined.

Multiple regression equations were computed for each of the four principal creativity tests, with verbal IQ, reading achievement, mathematical IQ, mathematical achievement, and gender as predictor variables. It was decided to remove variance attributable to gender because, to the extent that gender-related differences existed, it would be difficult to interpret their effects in terms of a general creativity-relevant skill. Table 4.4 shows the amount of variance accounted for by each of these regression equations. $R^2$ values ranged from .22 for the equation-creating test ($p < .05$; adjusted $R^2 = .13$) to .31 for the word-problem-creating test ($p < .01$; adjusted $R^2 = .24$).

Table 4.5 lists the partial correlations using the residual variance, after removing variance shared with the several standardized test scores, among the four principal creativity tests and the verbal-fluency test. There were only two significant correlations, one in the predicted direction (story-verbal fluency; $r = .38$, $p < .01$) and one

**TABLE 4.3**

Zero-Order Correlations of Creativity and Standardized Test Scores (Study 1)

| Test | Poetry | Story | Word Problem | Equation | Verbal Fluency | Verbal IQ | Reading Achievement | Math IQ | Math Achievement |
|---|---|---|---|---|---|---|---|---|---|
| Poetry | 1.00 | | | | | | | | |
| Story | .23 | 1.00 | | | | | | | |
| Word problem | .31* | .20 | 1.00 | | | | | | |
| Equation | −.14 | −.03 | −.20 | 1.00 | | | | | |
| Verbal fluency | .08 | .34* | −.19 | .09 | 1.00 | | | | |
| Verbal IQ | .44** | .45** | .38** | .00 | −.06 | 1.00 | | | |
| Reading achievement | .39** | .37** | .36** | .04 | −.02 | .60** | 1.00 | | |
| Math IQ | .16 | .14 | .51** | .27 | −.28* | .45** | .32* | 1.00 | |
| Math achievement | .18 | .09 | .26 | .28** | −.08 | .48** | .49** | .39** | 1.00 |

*Note.* $N = 50$.
*$p < .05$ two-tailed. **$p < .01$ two-tailed.

TABLE 4.4
Creativity Test Variance Accounted for by Standardized
Test Scores (Study 1)

| Test | $R^2$ | Adjusted $R^2$ |
|------|-------|----------------|
| Poetry | .23* | .14 |
| Story | .26* | .18 |
| Word problem | .31** | .24 |
| Equation | .22* | .13 |

*Note.* Standardized tests include verbal IQ, reading achievement, math IQ, and math achievement.
*$p < .05$ two-tailed ($df = 5,45$). **$p < .01$ two-tailed ($df = 5,45$).

TABLE 4.5
Partial Correlations Among Creativity Tests[a] (Study 1)

| Test | Poetry | Story | Word Problem | Equation | Verbal Fluency |
|------|--------|-------|--------------|----------|----------------|
| Poetry | 1.00 | − .01 | .19 | − .14 | .10 |
| Story | | 1.00 | .05 | .07 | .38* |
| Word problem | | | 1.00 | − .45* | − .06 |
| Equation | | | | 1.00 | .26 |

*Note.* $N = 50$.
[a]Correlations of residual variance after variance attributable to standardized test scores (verbal IQ, reading achievement, math IQ, math achievement) and gender have been removed.
*$p < .01$ two-tailed.

in the opposite direction (word problem-equation; $r = -.45, p < .01$). In all other cases, the correlations were low, and the only one that approached statistical significance was the correlation between equation-creating and verbal fluency, in which $p < .10$.

Finally, semi-partial regression coefficients were computed for each of the four principal creativity tests, using the four standardized test scores, gender, and the verbal-fluency test. This analysis was not motivated by any of the experimental hypotheses, but was done to see what clues it might offer to unique contributions to creative performance in each of the tasks. The results are presented in Table 4.6. Verbal IQ was a significant predictor of story-writing creativity (unique $R^2 = .09$, $p < .05$) and a marginally significant predictor of poetry-writing creativity (unique $R^2 = .07, p < .10$); mathematical IQ was a significant predictor of word-problem-creating creativity scores (unique $R^2 = .11, p < .05$); and mathematical achievement was a significant predictor of equation-creating creativity ($R^2 = .08, p < .05$). Verbal fluency contributed uniquely in predicting only story-writing creativity ($R^2 = .12$, $p < .01$). It is interesting to note that gender accounted uniquely for less than 0.2% (.002) of the variance on all the tests except writing math equations, where it accounted for 8% (.08) of the variance ($p < .05$).

## Discussion of Study 1

The primary hypothesis of Study 1—that creative performance on tasks in one

TABLE 4.6
Significant Semi-Partial Regression Coefficients[a] (Study 1)

| Creativity Test | Predictor Test | Unique $R^2$ | F | p |
|---|---|---|---|---|
| Poetry | Verbal IQ | .071 | 4.01 | < .10 |
| Story | Verbal IQ | .092 | 6.43 | < .05 |
| Story | Verbal fluency | .124 | 8.66 | < .01 |
| Word problem | Math IQ | .107 | 6.74 | < .05 |
| Equations | Math achievement | .092 | 5.49 | < .05 |
| Equations | Gender[b] | .080 | 4.77 | < .05 |

*Note.* All possible semi-partial regression coefficients were computed, but only those with $p < .10$ or better were reported. Two-tailed tests of significance; $df = 1,43$.

[a]Semi-partial regression coefficients derived from multiple regression using standardized test scores (verbal IQ, reading achievement, math IQ, math achievement), gender, and verbal-fluency test score.

[b]Males scored higher than females.

domain would not predict creativity on tasks in other domains—received strong support from this study. The results did not suggest, however, that there are intra-domain creative-thinking skills that are relevant to performance on any task within a domain, at least within the broadly defined domains of verbal and mathematical creativity, as predicted by the second hypothesis. Rather than pointing to creative-thinking skills that are widely applicable within the domains of Gardner's (1983, 1988) linguistic and logical-mathematical intelligences, the results suggest much more narrowly defined domains—possibly as narrow as the constraints of the specific tasks.

The third hypothesis of Study 1, that verbal fluency would be correlated with verbal creativity but not with mathematical creativity, received only qualified support. Because this was a single-item test, any findings related to this measure must be considered, at best, tentative. It is interesting that the verbal-fluency test was not correlated with either the verbal IQ or reading achievement tests, however. This is in line with previous research that shows a statistical separation of divergent- and convergent-thinking test scores from nursery school through college using the Wallach and Kogan (1965a) tasks, although research using other divergent-thinking tests often does not shown such a separation (Kogan, 1983).

The results of Study 1 suggest, as predicted, that general, domain-independent creative-thinking skills like divergent thinking are not important in creative performance across a variety of task domains—at least across the verbal and mathematical domains of the tasks used in this study. The results also question the existence of creative-thinking skills that span either of the commonly defined domains of verbal and mathematical intelligence, at least among highly able eighth-grade students like those who participated in this study.

The sample used in the study was very restricted (highly able eighth-grade students), and because of the relationships among (a) standardized achievement and ability test scores, and (b) creativity test scores, the narrow range of abilities sampled would be expected to reduce correlations among the creativity test scores.

Studies 2–5 were basically replications of Study 1 using subjects of different ages, wider ability ranges among subjects, and some procedural modifications.

## STUDIES 2-5: REPLICATIONS AND EXTENSIONS

Because these studies are essentially replications of Study 1 with different age groups and tasks, the studies are described in somewhat less detail.

### Study 2: Fourth-Grade Students

The primary purpose of Study 2 was to replicate Study 1 using (a) a younger sample, and (b) a sample with less restricted ranges of measured IQ and achievement. The same five creativity tests used in Study 1 were employed and the procedures were similar. The hypothesis was that scores on the five creativity tests, after removal of the variance accounted for by standardized achievement and ability tests, would be negligible. The sample was quite small for a correlational study ($N = 19$); however, as one piece in a growing picture, the results are nonetheless informative.

Method

*Subjects*

The entire fourth grade of a small, suburban school in southern New Jersey participated in Study 2. There were 19 students in the class, 10 girls and 9 boys. Standardized IQ and achievement testing, which followed the creativity testing, indicated that the range of IQ and achievement test scores was not as great as had been anticipated, based on the results of standardized tests that the students had taken in previous years. For example, IQ test scores ranged only from 100 to 146 on the Otis-Lennon School Ability Index, with a mean score of 120 and a standard deviation of 11.9. Overall, this sample represents a somewhat greater range of standardized test score variability than was found among the subjects of Study 1, but it is still limited to students scoring in the average and above-average range.

*Tests*

The five creativity tests were essentially the same as those used in Study 1, with minor modifications in how one of the tasks was presented to students to make that task more appropriate for this younger group (as explained in more detail in the following Procedure section).

The standardized tests employed were the Otis-Lennon School Ability Index, the Total Reading Achievement score of the California Achievement Test, and the Total Math Achievement score of the California Achievement Test. All of these standardized tests were given within four months following creativity testing.

## Procedure

Students were tested in their regular classroom in the same manner as in Study 1. The classroom teacher was present during the testing and cooperated with all procedures and arrangements, but she did not directly participate in the testing.

Because the equation-creating task, as originally conceived, was more applicable to students studying algebra than to students studying fourth-grade mathematics, it was presented in Study 2 as a "This Equals That" game. The experimenter's explanation of this task, which included a few very simple examples, was given in a considerably less sophisticated manner than in Study 1. The basic task, however, was the same.

## Results and Discussion

The mean IQ test score was 120.5, with a standard deviation of 11.9. The mean Total Reading Achievement percentile score was 79.2, with a standard deviation of 14.5. The mean Total Math Achievement percentile score was 82.2, with a standard deviation of 10.8

Interrater reliabilities of the four creativity tests that were rated by judges were satisfactory (poetry writing = .79; story writing = .88; word problem creating = .69; and equation creating = .91). As in Study 1 (and in all subsequent studies), the judges did not know the subjects, nor did they know the purpose of the study. Instructions given to judges can be found in Appendix A, and a description of judges can be found in Appendix B.

Because of the small sample size, a less extensive analysis of the data was conducted than in Study 1. There were no significant correlations among the creativity tests. The IQ test was significantly correlated with the reading achievement test ($r = .52, p < .05$) and the poetry-writing test ($r = .56, p < .05$). The reading achievement test was also significantly correlated with the poetry-writing test ($r = .57, p < .05$). The full list of zero-order correlation coefficients can be found in Table 4.7.

The important correlations from Table 4.7 for this study are those among the five creativity tests. These are small, and 4 of the 10 are negative. There is little evidence, once again, of the effects of any general creative-thinking skill or skills. As in Study 1, however, a better analysis can be made after removing the variance in the creativity test scores attributable to achievement and ability indices (the IQ, reading achievement, and math achievement test scores). This was done in a similar manner to the procedure followed in Study 1.

Partial correlations of residual variance (after variance shared by the several standardized test scores has been removed) among the five creativity tests are listed in Table 4.8. Half are positive and half are negative. Although one would not expect many statistically significant findings in a sample this small, even if one ignores significance levels and looks only at the obtained correlations, the overall pattern does not suggest anything but randomness. This lack of correlations among the various creativity tests again suggests

TABLE 4.7
Zero-Order Correlations of Creativity and Standardized Test Scores (Study 2)

| Test | Poetry | Story | Word Problem | Equation | Verbal Fluency | IQ | Reading Achievement | Math Achievement |
|---|---|---|---|---|---|---|---|---|
| Poetry | 1.00 | −.04 | .14 | .03 | .16 | .56* | .57* | .14 |
| Story | | 1.00 | .26 | −.24 | −.05 | −.18 | .01 | −.43 |
| Word problem | | | 1.00 | −.07 | .07 | −.21 | −.09 | .02 |
| Equation | | | | 1.00 | .28 | .35 | −.09 | .09 |
| Verbal fluency | | | | | 1.00 | .28 | .36 | .05 |
| IQ | | | | | | 1.00 | .52* | .42 |
| Reading achievement | | | | | | | 1.00 | .28 |
| Math achievement | | | | | | | | 1.00 |

Note. $N = 19$.
*$p < .05$ two-tailed.

TABLE 4.8
Partial Correlation Among Creativity Tests[a] (Study 2)

| Test | Poetry | Story | Word Problem | Equation | Verbal Fluency |
|------|--------|-------|--------------|----------|----------------|
| Poetry | 1.00 | −.05 | .39 | −.10 | .13 |
| Story | | 1.00 | .29 | −.26 | −.10 |
| Word problem | | | 1.00 | −.09 | .05 |
| Equation | | | | 1.00 | .21 |

Note. N = 19.
[a]Correlations of residual variance after variance attributable to standardized test scores (IQ, reading achievement, math achievement) and gender have been removed.

that general creative-thinking skills—at least any such skills for which one would expect variability across individuals—are not in evidence in the products of these fourth-grade students.

## Study 3: Fifth-Grade Students

Study 3 used the same 19 subjects from Study 2. Its primary purposes were (a) to assess the stability of creativity test scores over a fairly long period, and (b) to demonstrate thereby that the essentially random pattern of correlations obtained in earlier studies—and, as it turned out, in Studies 4–7—were not due primarily to the unreliability of the tests.

Subjects were retested using two of the tests (poetry writing and story writing) 11 months later, as fifth-grade students. Instructions were the same for the tests in the previous year, but the prompts—the topic of the poem, and the picture on which the story was to be based—were different. As in Studies 1 and 2, inter-rater reliabilities were measured using the alpha coefficient, and they were adequate for the purpose: poetry writing = .76, story writing = .85.

There was considerable stability in test scores on the same tests given almost a year later (test–retest correlations: $r$ = .44 for poetry-writing creativity, $p$ < .10; $r$ = .58 for story-writing creativity, $p$ < .01, two-tailed tests). Although not as high as the stability coefficients commonly found in IQ test scores, these levels are in the same range as comparable coefficients measuring long-term stability of divergent-thinking test scores (Kogan, 1983), and they appear to be quite adequate for the purposes of the studies reported here. Because of the extended interval between testings, these one-year-later test–retest correlations are not a good measure of test–retest reliability; in fact, one would expect considerably higher test–retest reliability over a shorter time period. This suggests that the performance-based consensual assessment technique being employed has considerable test–retest reliability, at least for the poetry-writing and story-writing tests. (More evidence to this effect is presented in connection with Studies 5 and 7, which appear later.)

The results are also of interest as partial replication of the basic outcomes of Studies 1 and 2. The sample, again, is quite small for a correlational study; however, the results provide an additional piece to what is beginning to become a consistent pattern. The zero-order correlation between scores on the two tests was .04. After removing variance accounted for by the IQ and achievement tests (using the same standardized tests employed in Study 2, tests that were given during the previous school year and which were approximately 7 months old at the time of the creativity testing for Study 3), the resulting partial correlation increased slightly to .08. The observed absence of a relationship between creativity scores on the two different tasks follows the same pattern observed in Studies 1 and 2, once again suggesting the absence or near absence of the effects of any general creative-thinking skills (such as divergent thinking).

## Study 4: Second-Grade Students

The purpose of Study 4 was to replicate partially and to extend the results of Studies 1, 2, and 3 using a younger sample, different tasks, and a streamlined rating procedure. (A second purpose of Study 4 is considered in chapter 5, in connection with Studies 6 and 7.) A group of 38 second-grade students each made a collage and told a story based on a picture book. There was only one hypothesis: that experts' ratings of the creativity on the two tasks would not be correlated.

### Method

#### Subjects

Thirty-eight second-grade students—the entire second grade of a small suburban elementary school in southern New Jersey—served as subjects. California Achievement Test scores were above average in both reading and mathematics, although there was a wide range of achievement that roughly approximated a normal distribution of test scores. One student came to the school just prior to the time when these tests were given and had therefore not taken the same battery of standardized achievement tests, but of the 37 students who had taken the California Achievement Tests, the distribution of scores was as follows: *reading achievement*—15 in the top quartile, 13 in the second quartile, 8 in the third quartile, 1 in the lowest quartile; *math achievement*—8 in the top quartile, 17 in the second quartile, 11 in the third quartile, and 1 in the lowest quartile; *language arts skills*—9 in the top quartile, 19 in the second quartile, 6 in the third quartile, and 3 in the lowest quartile.

#### Tests

Two tests were used in this study, both of which have been used and validated extensively by Amabile (1982, 1983) and Hennessey and Amabile (1988b). In the collage-making task, subjects were given a blank 14" × 22" piece of white tagboard, a bottle of glue, and a set of over one hundred pre-cut construction paper designs (including hearts, butterflies, squares, circles, and triangles of various colors) and asked to make an "interesting, silly design." The materials each student received were identical. There was no time limit, but most students finished in less than 20 minutes. The collages were later rated for creativity by art educators.

In the storytelling test, subjects were shown a picture book, the same one used by Amabile (1983) in the studies she conducted to validate the procedure: *A Boy, a Dog, and a Frog* (Mayer, 1967). After looking through the book at their own pace to become familiar with the story, the students were instructed to "tell the story in your own words by saying one thing about each page" while looking at the book's pictures. These stories were later transcribed by the experimenter (except for two that were lost due to garbled speech in one case and tape recorder malfunction in the other) and given to experts to rate for creativity. The experimenter attempted to transcribe the verbal expressions and emphases that the students used in telling the stories as accurately as possible. On a few occasions, this was difficult because part of the flavor of the story was conveyed in the tone of voice used by the students, but for the most part, this transcription was a straightforward affair. Sample responses to a very similar picture book (used in Study 7) are included in Appendix C.

The rating procedure was different than the rank ordering used in Studies 1, 2, and 3. Judges simply rated each collage or story on a 1.00–5.00 scale. There were four judges for the storytelling test and 13 for the collage-making test. Instructions given to the judges can be found in Appendix A, and a description of the judges can be found in Appendix B.

### Procedure

Each student was tested individually. Prior to testing, the experimenter met with the students in two class groups and explained what they would be doing. When students met individually with the experimenter, he asked them about their family ("Do you have any brothers and sisters?") and the weather ("Are you hoping for snow?" "What do you like to do when it snows?") briefly to make the students more comfortable.

The students had little trouble understanding the tasks. Their teachers reported that all made collages before. Some students were shy before starting to tell the story. When this happened, they were prompted to "just say one thing about each page."

The order of tasks was reversed for every other student. The collages made by previous subjects were out of view of the subjects as they worked on their collages. The students were told that they would be given their collages to keep "sometime next month," a promise that was, of course, kept.

### Results and Discussion of Study 4

Because two of the storytelling tests were unusable (as explained earlier), the result was $N = 36$. Alpha coefficient interrater reliabilities were very good: .90 for the storytelling test and .91 for the collage-making test.

Only a single statistical analysis was conducted—a correlation between creativity scores on the two tests. Although not statistically significant ($p < .20$) nor very large ($r = .21$), this modest correlation is difficult to evaluate by itself. A true correlation of .21 would mean that 4.4% (.044) of the variance in the two creativity test scores was shared, and thus attributable to a common source. Part or all of that 4.4% could reflect the contribution of general creative-thinking skills such as divergent thinking; on the other hand, factors other than general creative-thinking skills (such as some kind of verbal intelligence, or task motivation) could have caused all of the shared variance.

The possibility that task motivation might have systematically influenced the subjects' performance is greater in this study than in Studies 1–3, because subjects did not all take the tests together or at the same time, and they in fact took the tests in a rather unusual situation—in a room next to the school nurse's office, where they worked alone with the experimenter, a man who was not (at that time) very well known to the subjects. At least three factors— (a) doing the tasks at different times and on different days, (b) being pulled out of different activities to take the tests, and (c) experiencing different reactions to the unusual testing situation due to personality differences—might have led to different levels of anxiety, different degrees of a desire to please the experimenter, different expectations regarding evaluation of their work, and so on among the students. These are all factors that could have systematically influenced creative performance (Amabile, 1983) and could therefore have caused the observed correlation between the two tests.

Because of the relatively small sample size (which makes it impossible to reject the null hypothesis that there is a significant correlation, and also difficult to estimate the size of the true correlation) and the fact that only two tests were given (which allows only a single correlation to be computed), this outcome must be considered inconclusive. Compared to the zero-order correlations among creativity tests in Studies 1, 2, and 3, this figure is fairly high, although there were in those studies several other correlations this high (both positive and negative). In Studies 1–3, occasional positive correlations of this magnitude could be discounted because complementary correlations among other creativity tests yielded either near-zero or negative correlations. The results of Study 4 do not clearly show whether second-grade students use general creative-thinking processes in creativity-relevant tasks like telling stories and making collages, although they do suggest the possibility of a modest contribution by such general creative-thinking skills with these younger subjects. Further information about these same subjects at a later testing date is presented as a part of Study 7 (in chapter 5). In that study, the effects of any general creative-thinking skills were even less in evidence.

## Study 5: Adults

The purposes of this study were (a) to replicate partially and extend the results of Studies 1, 2, and 3, using an adult sample, and (b) to attempt a version of alternate-forms reliability of the poetry-writing test. All previous studies used fairly young students, as would Studies 6 and 7. Study 5 was conducted to assess the general extent to which the results of Studies 1–4 might be generalizable to older populations.

All subjects wrote two poems and one story. Based on the results of Studies 1–4, it was predicted that there would be a near-zero correlation between creativity scores on the poetry- and story-writing tests, but that there would be a significant correlation between the two poetry-writing tests

## Method

### Subjects

Participants were 27 students at a 2-year college in the mid-Atlantic region. All were students in an English Composition class. They ranged in age from 18 to 42, with a mean age of 28. This is somewhat older than a typical sample of first-year college students, reflecting the fact that this study was conducted in an evening class at a community college.

### Tests

Each subject wrote, on three separate occasions, two poems and one short story. The tasks were the same as those used in Studies 1–3, with different topics used for the two poems. These poems and stories were rated by three separate groups of experts for creativity on a 1.00–5.00 scale, as in Study 4. There were only three judges for each poem or story; all were college English professors who worked alone and who did not know the students. One of the three judges in each of the two groups of poetry judges was also a published poet, and one of the short-story judges was a fiction writer. See Appendices A and B for instructions given to judges and a general description of the judges.

### Procedure

All three tasks were presented as ungraded free-writing activities that were introduced by the professor as "warm-up" activities for the class. The first poem and the story were written early in the semester. The second poem was written about 10 weeks later.

## Results and Discussion

The correlation between creativity scores on the first poetry-writing test and the story-writing test was .07 The correlation between creativity scores on the second poetry-writing test and the story-writing test was .32. Neither of these correlations approached statistical significance, although the .32 result was higher predicted and cannot be lightly dismissed simply because it did not reach statistical significance. As was the case in Study 4, the combination of small sample size and the use of only a small number of tests makes the results somewhat difficult to interpret, although the evidence for a general creative-thinking skill underlying these performances is, at best, rather thin. In the case of one of two poetry-writing tests, a modest correlation was discovered with story-writing creativity, suggesting the possibility of a common mediating factor, such as some general creative-thinking skill; but the absence of even a modest correlation between the story-writing and the other poetry-writing test, which was conducted at a point closer in time to the story-writing test, makes this weak support, at best, for such a conclusion.

The correlation between the two poetry-writing test scores was .65, an acceptable alternate-forms reliability. This figure would probably have been even higher had both tests been conducted at the same time. Amabile (1983) showed that creativity tests are easily influenced by motivational constraints, especially those having to do with expectations of evaluation. Although subjects had been assured that both of the poems and the story would not be evaluated for grading purposes, the salience of evaluation can be influenced by factors other than knowledge regarding the possibility of such evaluation (Amabile, 1983). Because the two samples were taken at different times (with a 10-week interval between them), the classroom atmosphere vis-à-vis the salience of evaluation at the different testings may have been different. This would lower the expected correlation between scores on tests taken at different times to the extent that subjects taking the tests are influenced by different motivational constraints at different testings. It should be noted that the possibility of differing motivational effects due to testing at different times could also have lowered the correlations between story-writing and poetry-writing creativity. For research of this kind, every effort needs to be made to ensure that testing circumstances do not vary from test to test. In light of this constraint, doing all testing at the same time is preferable when possible.[1]

---

[1]A correction for attenuation can be used to estimate the extent to which observed correlations are attenuated by measurement error (Cohen & Cohen, 1983; Nunnally, 1978). To the extent that measurements are unreliable, correlations between those measures will be lessened, and an estimate can be made of what the correlation would have been if perfectly reliable measures had been used. The formula is:

$$\text{predicted } r_{12} = \frac{\text{observed } r_{12}}{\text{square root of } (r_{11} \times r_{22})}$$

There is some controversy about when this should be applied (Cohen & Cohen, 1983; Nunnally, 1978), and as it would have little effect on most of the correlations reported in Studies 1–4 (see pages 65 and 66), I have waited until this point to introduce the possibility of making better estimates of the observed correlations. The magnitude of the effect increases with the unreliability of the measures, and, as the reliabilities for the most part are quite good (and at the worst still in an acceptable range), the impact is small. The magnitude of the effect also increases with the size of the correlation, however. With a correlation as high as that found between the two tests of poetry-writing creativity (.65) in Study 5 (see page 66), the correction for attenuation would yield a .73 estimate of the true correlation between these two tests, despite the fact that the inter-rater reliabilities of both tests were quite high (.86 and .92).

Similarly, the 1-year stability scores reported in Study 3 for the poetry- and story-writing creativity tests would each be increased substantially. The estimate of the true correlation between the two measures of poetry-writing creativity jumps from .44 to .57, and the estimate of the true correlation between the two measures of story-writing creativity jumps from .58 to .67.

Because the correlations themselves are generally much smaller, the effect of applying the correction for attenuation formula to the correlations between different creativity tests scores is less. The effect on the interpretation of the results is minimal, because almost half of the original correlations were negative, so the changes produce slightly larger positive and slightly larger negative correlations. There is little change in the overall pattern, or in the general conclusion that there is little evidence of the influence of general creative-thinking skills such as divergent thinking. To be complete, however, the changes would be as follows in the tables on pages 65 and 66.

There is some evidence from other research with adult populations for domain-transcending creative-thinking skills. Sternberg and Lubart (1991) asked 48 adult subjects (mean age = 33.4 years) to produce eight products: two drawings, two stories, two advertisements, and two scientific problem solutions. Cross-task correlations of creativity scores for these products ranged from .23 to .61, with a median correlation of .42 ($p < .01$). Although these correlations are quite a bit higher than might be predicted by the results of Studies 1–5, there are several possible explanations for this difference.

Of greatest importance is the ways the products were judged. Sternberg and Lubart (1991) employed Amabile's (1982, 1983) consensual assessment technique —basically the same technique for rating the creativity of products used in all the studies (1–7) reported here. However, rather than using expert judges for each task, the same raters judged all eight products. This presents two problems. First, there is the question of the judges' expertise. And second, there is the problem of spurious correlations arising because judges' stylistic preferences might be consistent across

### STUDY 1
#### (Zero-Order Correlations)

| Tests | Change from | to |
|---|---|---|
| Poetry–Story | .23 | .26 |
| Poetry–Word problem | .31 | .38 |
| Poetry–Equation | −.14 | −.16 |
| Story–Word problem | .20 | .24 |
| Story–Equation | −.03 | −.03 |
| Word problem–Equation | −.20 | −.24 |

### STUDY 2

| Tests | Change from | to |
|---|---|---|
| Poetry–Story | −.04 | −.05 |
| Poetry–Word problem | .14 | .19 |
| Poetry–Equation | .03 | .04 |
| Story–Word problem | .26 | .33 |
| Story–Education | −.24 | −.31 |
| Word problem–Equation | −.07 | −.09 |

### STUDY 3

| Tests | Change from | to |
|---|---|---|
| Poetry–Story | .04 | .05 |

### STUDY 4

| Tests | Change from | to |
|---|---|---|
| Collage–Story | .21 | .23 |

tasks.

Also important is the fact that in the Sternberg and Lubart (1991) study, as in Study 5, no partial correlations were computed. In Study 5, appropriate test data were not available. In the Sternberg and Lubart study, a variety of measures of intellectual processes—including Cattell's Culture Fair Test of "g" (Cattell & Cattell, 1963) and Sternberg and Lubart's own test of intellectual processes (Sternberg & Lubart, 1991)—were employed, as well as a 33-item questionnaire that was used as a measure of general knowledge. Across task domains, fluid intelligence (as measured by Cattell's Culture-Fair Test of "g") was found to be the most important contributor to creativity, with correlations ranging from .51 to .61

### STUDY 5

| Tests | Change from | to |
|---|---|---|
| Poetry 1–Story | .07 | .08 |
| Poetry 2–Story | .32 | .35 |

### STUDY 6

| Tests | Change from | to |
|---|---|---|
| Collage–Story | .29 | .32 |

### STUDY 4 AND STUDY 7
#### (Zero-Order Correlations)

| Tests | Change | Total Group from | to | Control from | to | Experimental from | to |
|---|---|---|---|---|---|---|---|
| Storytelling 2–Story-writing | | .46 | .52 | .46 | .52 | .26 | .30 |
| Storytelling 2–Poetry | | .25 | .29 | .10 | .12 | .13 | .15 |
| Storytelling 2–Word problem | | − .11 | − .13 | − .42 | − .49 | .34 | .40 |
| Storytelling 2–Collage 2 | | .09 | .10 | − .02 | − .02 | .07 | .08 |
| Storytelling 2–Storytelling 1 | | .48 | .55 | .37 | .43 | .63 | .72 |
| Storytelling 2–Collage 1 | | .15 | .17 | .18 | .20 | .42 | .48 |
| Story-writing–Poetry | | .31 | .34 | .01 | .01 | .16 | .18 |
| Story-writing–Word problem | | − .12 | − .13 | − .25 | − .28 | .22 | .24 |
| Story-writing–Collage 2 | | .04 | .04 | − .35 | − .39 | .29 | .32 |
| Story-writing–Storytelling 1 | | .37 | .41 | .57 | .63 | .10 | .11 |
| Story-writing–Collage 1 | | − .22 | − .24 | .02 | .02 | − .24 | − .26 |
| Poetry–Word problem | | − .03 | − .03 | .01 | .01 | .10 | .11 |
| Poetry–Collage 2 | | .26 | .30 | .39 | .45 | − .02 | − .02 |
| Poetry–Storytelling 1 | | .04 | .04 | .01 | .01 | .02 | .02 |
| Poetry–Collage 1 | | .17 | .19 | .48 | .54 | .33 | .37 |
| Word problem–Collage 2 | | .02 | .02 | .09 | .10 | − .01 | − .01 |
| Word problem–Storytelling 1 | | − .12 | − .13 | − .37 | − .42 | .24 | .27 |
| Word problem–Collage 1 | | .30 | .34 | .18 | .20 | .46 | .52 |
| Collage 2–Storytelling 1 | | − .25 | − .28 | − .22 | − .25 | − .32 | − .36 |
| Collage 2–Collage 1 | | .13 | .15 | .43 | .48 | − .01 | − .01 |
| Storytelling 1–Collage 1 | | .21 | .23 | .09 | .10 | .39 | .43 |

(in all cases, $p < .001$). This was followed closely by the test of knowledge, which also produced a median correlation with the various task domains above .50 ($p < .001$). It is likely that the observed correlations among creativity test scores across task domains were due to differences in these intellectual processing and knowledge resources. These factors parallel the IQ and achievement test scores that were used in Studies 1–4 to compute partial correlations, after the variance attributable to those factors had been removed. Because they were focusing on different issues, however, Sternberg and Lubart have not done the partial correlations of their data that would answer this question (R. J. Sternberg, personal communication, September 21, 1991).

It is, therefore, unclear how far the results of Studies 1–4 can be generalized in regard to adult populations. If it could be shown that a general skill emerges late in the course of cognitive development, this would be a very interesting contrast to typical developmental patterns, in which increasing differentiation of function is the general rule (McShane, 1991). However, the evidence supporting such an interpretation is, at present, still quite weak.

## General Discussion of Studies 1–5

The fairly consistent pattern of results obtained in these five studies makes a strong case for an absence of any significant effects of general creative-thinking skills on the performance of a wide range of subjects on a variety of creativity-relevant tasks. As discussed earlier, this contradicts many current theories of creativity that posit such general creativity-relevant skills (Draper, 1985; Hennessey & Amabile, 1988a; Simon, 1967; Tardif & Sternberg, 1988; Torrance & Presbury, 1984; Treffinger, 1986).

The results also fail to support a theory of modular creative-thinking skills that operate within broadly defined cognitive domains, as suggested by Gardner (1983, 1988). Two of the tests used in Studies 1, 2, 3, and 5 (the poetry-writing and story-writing tasks) would be classified as primarily verbal-domain tasks; however, creativity ratings on these tests appear to share no creativity-relevant skill that is distinct from general domain competence (as measured by IQ and achievement tests)— at least in Studies 1–3, with somewhat more equivocal results in Study 5. In fact, creativity scores on these two tasks share little variance of any kind, including that tapped by IQ and achievement tests, as evidenced by the comparison of the zero-order and partial correlations in Studies 1–3. A similar pattern is true of the equation-creating and mathematical word-problem-creating tests used in Studies 1 and 2, although these are less exclusively from the same cognitive domain.

Studies 1–5 present a serious challenge to any theory of creativity claiming that general creative-thinking skills are important factors contributing to creative performance. Divergent-thinking theories of creativity make precisely this claim— that skill in divergent thinking is a general cognitive skill or set of skills that contributes to creative performance in any task domain. Even if divergent-thinking theories and divergent-thinking tests are limited to domain-specific interpretations (e.g., using the Torrance verbal tests only to predict creative performance in the verbal domain, and the Torrance figural tests only to predict creativity in the spatial domain), the results of Studies 1–5 suggest that domain-wide creative-thinking skills are also not significant contributors to creativity. In sum, Studies 1–5 appear to directly contradict the claim that divergent thinking is a significant contributor to creativity, either as a single divergent-thinking skill or as several domain-relevant divergent-thinking skills.

The tests of creativity used in the studies reported here have a "real world" flavor, but, of course, no test is without limitations. The tests were all assigned and administered in a school setting, and school environments may result in different kinds of creative performance than would be found in other settings. Just as the observed lack of correlation among creativity scores argues against the importance of general creative-thinking skills, future work may find a similar lack of correlation among creative performances on similar tasks undertaken in different (i.e., nonschool) settings.

There is also the problem of predicting population behaviors based on small samples of subjects. The results of the studies are sufficiently consistent, however, to allow a fairly confident statement that, at least for fourth-grade through eighth-grade students working in school settings (and very probably for second-grade and college students as well), creative performance on tasks such as writing poems and stories and creating mathematical word problems and equations is little influenced by general creative-thinking skills or heuristics such as divergent thinking.

# 5

# Evaluations of the Effects of Training in Divergent Thinking on Creative Performance

Divergent thinking is a skill that everyone has available to some degree, and divergent-thinking test results indicate that the level of such skill varies considerably among individuals. If divergent thinking were a skill that influenced creative performance across task domains, it should consistently produce positive correlations among tests of creative performances of individuals across different tasks, but this was not found to be true in Studies 1–5. These outcomes are difficult to explain in terms of standard divergent-thinking theories of creativity. However, if subjects do indeed possess varying degrees of skill in divergent-thinking, but do not use that skill in appropriate situations (due, perhaps, to lack of training), then the lack of correlations could be explained within the framework of the revised divergent-thinking theory proposed in chapter 2.

According to this revised divergent-thinking theory of creativity, it is possible that divergent thinking may play an important role in creative performance if one knows when to use it, but because most people have had no explicit training in when to apply such skill, they simply do not produce it at appropriate times. By separating competence in divergent thinking from performance (especially the metacognitive strategy of knowing when to apply divergent thinking in creativity-relevant situations), the revised divergent-thinking theory of creativity could explain the results of Studies 1–5, which used subjects with no training in divergent thinking.

This revised divergent-thinking theory would also predict very different outcomes of studies similar to Studies 1–5, but conducted using subjects trained in divergent-thinking skills and techniques. One of the goals of Studies 6 and 7 was to test this revised divergent-thinking theory of creativity.

As noted in chapter 3, there are many creativity-training programs, and most of these programs emphasize divergent thinking. One explicit goal of such training is to increase the availability of divergent-thinking skills; however, Studies 1–5 suggest that increasing the availability of divergent-thinking skills alone will not result in increased creativity across task domains. Divergent-thinking training approaches to increasing creativity also demonstrate when to apply such skill, however, even when they do not give explicit, separate instruction regarding its application. They may do this narrowly, focusing on only a specific kind of problem (e.g., Covington, Crutchfield, Davies, & Olton, 1974), or broadly, teaching how to apply divergent thinking to a wide range of creativity-relevant problems (e.g., Parnes & Noller, 1973).

Unfortunately, no divergent-thinking training program's effect on creative performance has been evaluated in a way that (a) assesses creative performance using creative products, rather than divergent-thinking tests, (b) separates divergent-thinking training from other components of creativity training, and (c) tests creative performance in domains different from those practiced in training. Making this kind of thorough evaluation of the effects of divergent-thinking training on actual creative performance was another goal of Studies 6 and 7.

Of course, it is possible that divergent-thinking training might improve creative performance across task domains but still not result in correlations among creativity test scores. This might happen if training programs in divergent thinking did not, as is commonly assumed, consist primarily of intensive training in a single, easily transferable skill or set of skills.

An alternate conception of what happens in divergent-thinking training is that participants are trained in a wide diversity of unrelated skills— skills that only seem related because we describe them in similar terms (including both the way that we state these skills in terms of fluency, flexibility, or originality and the fact that we lump them together under the umbrella term *divergent thinking*). These skills might, in fact, be totally independent of one another on a cognitive performance level. Under this conception of divergent thinking, each such skill would be applicable only to a narrow range of tasks, and there could be little or no transfer of these skills from one task to another.

The two aforementioned goals are, then, in a sense, listed in reverse order. That is, if the second goal (which in effect asks the question, "Does training in divergent thinking have a positive impact on creative performance?") should result in a negative answer, there would be no point in pursuing the question raised by the first goal (which explores the nature of the effect of divergent-thinking training on creative performance, and therefore assumes that there is an impact of some kind). Only if the answer to the question, "Is there a positive impact?" is affirmative (which, to let one cat out of the bag, we see later that it was, especially in Study 7) does it make sense to investigate the nature of that impact, with the goal of determining how we might best understand and explain the observed influence of divergent thinking on creative performance.

The general design of Studies 6 and 7 was to compare two groups, one trained in divergent thinking and the other without such training, to see if the training resulted in more creative performance on a variety of tasks. Then, if (and only if) divergent-thinking training was found to have a positive effect on creative performance, correlations among creativity scores in diverse domains would be investigated to determine (a) if the effect were a general one, suggesting that a single underlying factor or set of factors caused the improvement in creative performance, or (b) if the effect were not a general one, suggesting that the observed effects were the result of many diverse, task-specific factors.

## Study 6: A Preliminary Investigation

Study 4 was, in fact, part of a larger study, and the results reported in Study 4 were those of the control group for Study 6. It was an opportunistic study in the sense that it used predetermined groups and an experimental treatment that had already occurred, in an uncontrolled environment, for purposes unrelated to the present research. Study 6 also lacked any direct control over the exact content of the treatment, which was a creativity enhancement program that was offered in one school to all primary students on an occasional basis.

These are rather large caveats, and the results of Study 6 must be understood in this context. At the same time, the results of Study 6 help to provide a context in which to interpret the results of the better controlled experimental study that followed it. One important objective of Study 6 was, in fact, to provide information about how to go about designing a well-controlled study of the effects of divergent-thinking training using a similar population from a different school.

The experimental group was a second-grade class at a school in the same district as the control group (matched for socioeconomic level and scholastic achievement) at which occasional training in divergent thinking had been given to all students in kindergarten, first grade, and the first few months of second grade prior to testing. The goal was to compare the performance of the two groups on two creativity-relevant tasks—telling stories and creating collages—to assess the effects of divergent-thinking training. The Torrance Test of Creative Thinking Figural Form A was also administered to both groups to measure divergent-thinking skill, although its interpretation with subjects who have had divergent-thinking training is problematic, as will be explained later. The Torrance test was given primarily as evidence that the standard effect of training in divergent thinking—an increase in divergent-thinking test scores—had indeed occurred. The Torrance test also provides a link between this study and most of the creativity-training studies in the literature (Kogan, 1983; Rose & Lin, 1984; Torrance & Presbury, 1974).

There were two predictions, based on the revised divergent-thinking theory of creativity:

1. The experimental group should score higher than the control group on both creative-performance tests (storytelling and collage making).

2. The correlation between the two creative-performance test scores should be higher for the experimental group than the control group. Because (a) subjects in the experimental group were expected to apply divergent thinking to both tasks, whereas (b) subjects in the control group, having had no training in when to apply divergent thinking, were expected not to do so, individual differences in divergent-thinking skill should, in the experimental group, result in systematic individual differences on all creativity-relevant tasks. This is another way of saying that the

hypothesis that scores on one creative performance test should be predictive of scores on tests of creative performance in other task domains— the hypothesis that was disconfirmed in Studies 1–5 for groups without divergent-thinking training— should be true of the experimental group, but not the control group.

## Method

### Subjects

The control group is described in Study 4. There were 37 second-grade students in the experimental group—the entire second grade of a small suburban elementary school in southern New Jersey. As with the control group, California Achievement Test scores were above average in both reading and mathematics, but with a wide range of achievement. The distribution of scores was as follows: *reading achievement*—17 in the top quartile, 11 in the second quartile, 4 in the third quartile, 4 in the lowest quartile; *mathematics achievement*—26 in the top quartile, 6 in the second quartile, 4 in the third quartile, and 0 in the lowest quartile; *language arts skills*—18 in the top quartile, 12 in the second quartile, 6 in the third quartile, and 1 in the lowest quartile. These achievement test scores are comparable to the control group's scores on the same tests (reported in Study 4). Other comparisons between the schools are summarized in Table 5.1.

### Tests

The tests were the same as those described in Study 4. The interrater reliabilities listed there are actually the interrater reliabilities for the total (experimental plus control) sample. All of the collages for both groups were rated by the same judges, and all of the stories were rated by the same judges. There was no overlap between the two sets of judges; that is, none of those who scored the collages scored the stories, and vice versa. The judges did not know the purpose of the study, nor did they know that there were two separate groups of subjects.

The Torrance Test of Creative Thinking Figural Form A was also administered to both groups. These tests were scored by the Torrance tests' paid scoring service.

### Procedure

This is described in Study 4. Testing of the two groups was done over the same

TABLE 5.1

Comparisons of the Control and Experimental Group Schools (Study 6)

| | School | |
| --- | --- | --- |
| *Basis of Comparison* | *Control* | *Experimental* |
| Yearly per pupil expenditures | $4,503 | $4,009 |
| Total enrollment | 261 | 193 |
| Student attendance | 95.5% | 95.7% |
| Student/professional ratio | 11.9 : 1 | 13.8 : 1 |

time period, on alternate days. The Torrance test of Creative Thinking Figural Form A was administered in small groups following standard Torrance test instructions. This test was given 2 months after the collage-making and story-telling tests, however, as a part of previously arranged school testing schedules. The Torrance tests were administered by school personnel. The collage-making and story telling tests were administered by the experimenter.

The creativity-enhancement training program, it might be noted, was basically the work of one person, the teacher responsible for the Talented and Gifted Program at the experimental-group school. She worked occasionally with kindergarten, first-grade, and second-grade classes, providing whole-class instruction in divergent thinking and other skills and activities designed to promote creative thinking. Her description of these activities indicated that most were standard divergent-thinking exercises, but she did not have a complete list or schedule of the activities she had conducted. The students in the experimental group had therefore received divergent-thinking training on an irregular schedule for over 2 years at the time of the testing conducted for Study 6.

## Results of Study 6

Because of garbled speech, two of the experimental group's stories could not be transcribed. The control group also lost two stories, as described in Study 4. For the collage-making task, $N = 75$, and for story-telling, $N = 71$, with one more subject in the control group than the experimental group in each case. Thirty-seven subjects in each group took the Torrance test.

As predicted, the experimental group scored higher than the control group on both of the creative-performance tests (storytelling and collage making), as well as on the test of divergent thinking (the Torrance test). The mean for the experimental group on the storytelling test (scored on a 1.00–5.00 scale) was 3.06, compared to 2.63 for the control group; $F(1,69) = 3.39$, $p < .10$. The mean for the experimental group on the collage-making test was 2.96, compared to 2.71 for the control group; $F(1,73) = 1.74$, $p < .20$. The Torrance test scores indicated that the training in divergent thinking had been very successful, as has generally been the case. (See Kogan, 1983, for a summary of the effects of various kinds of training on divergent thinking.) The experimental group had an average Torrance Test Creativity Index percentile score of 77.0, compared to the control group's 50.4: $F(1,72) = 18.91$, $p < .01$. These results are summarized in Table 5.2.

The correlation between collage-making and storytelling test scores was somewhat higher for subjects in the experimental group ($r = .29$, $p > .10$, two-tailed test) than the control group ($r = .21$, $p > .20$), although the difference between the two correlations was not statistically significant ($p < .20$). Table 5.3 summarizes the comparison of the correlations between the story-telling and collage-making creativity tests for the two schools. For the experimental group, the performance on one test accounted for 8.6% of the variance on the other test, which is twice as high as the percentage of shared variance on the two tests for the control group (4.3%).

TABLE 5.2
Creativity Test Comparisons (Study 6)

| Creativity Test | Group Mean | | F |
| | Control | Experimental | |
|---|---|---|---|
| Storytelling[a] | 2.63 | 3.06 | 3.39** (1,69) |
| | ($n = 36$) | ($n = 35$) | |
| Collage making[a] | 2.71 | 2.96 | 1.74* (1,73) |
| | ($n = 38$) | ($n = 37$) | |
| Torrance test[b] | 50.4 | 77.0 | 18.91*** (1,72) |
| | ($n = 37$) | ($n = 37$) | |

[a]1.00–5.00 scale.
[b]Percentile scores, Torrance Test of Creativity, Figural Form A, Creativity Index.
*$p < .20$ two-tailed. **$p < .10$ two-tailed. ***$p < .01$ two-tailed.

TABLE 5.3
Inter-Test Correlations (Study 6)

| Tests | Control | Experimental |
|---|---|---|
| Storytelling – Collage | .21 | .29* |
| Storytelling – Torrance test | – .05 | – .13 |
| Storytelling – Torrance test | – .13 | – .13 |

*$p < .10$ two-tailed.

The correlations between the two creative-performance tests and the Torrance test were in all four cases negative and small in number, ranging from -.05 to -.13. None of these correlations approached statistical significance. These correlations are also listed in Table 5.3.

## Discussion of Study 6

As predicted, the experimental group scored higher than the control group on both measures of creative performance and the divergent-thinking test. Although the differences on the two creative performance tasks (collage making and storytelling) were not highly significant statistically, both were higher in the predicted direction and both at least approached statistical significance. For these reasons, an interpretation of the results as providing modest support for the hypothesis that divergent-thinking training improves creative performance seems warranted.

This modest support for positive effects of divergent-thinking training allowed investigation of the follow-up hypothesis involving the revised divergent-thinking theory of creativity. Once again, the result was in the predicted direction—the correlation between collage-making and storytelling creativity was somewhat higher in the experimental group than in the control group—but the difference was not large, and there was little indication that the difference was more than a chance variation. (Using Fisher's z transformation [Cohen & Cohen, 1983] to compute the normal curve deviate, $z = .35$. Using a two-tailed test, a $z$ value of 1.28 would be needed to meet even a $p = .20$ criterion. Thus, the observed differences between the two correlation coefficients did not even approach statistical significance.)

Although the experimental group scored much higher on the Torrance test, indicating that training in divergent thinking did, indeed, improve their divergent-thinking ability, these scores were not correlated with either of the creative-performance measures. This lack of correlation between divergent-thinking test scores and creative-performance test scores in the experimental group appears to contradict the revised divergent-thinking of creativity (which, although not supported statistically by the comparison of correlations between collage-making and story-telling creativity scores, at least produced differences in these correlations, however small, in the predicted direction).

This failure of Torrance test scores to correlate with creativity test scores for the experimental group (as well as for the control group) should probably not be thought of as strong evidence against the revised divergent-thinking theory of creativity, however, because tests of divergent thinking have been shown to be unreliable when training is involved. Measures of divergent thinking are notorious for their susceptibility to score inflation resulting from (a) training (even brief training), (b) the conditions under which the tests are given, and (c) the specific directions given to subjects. For example, divergent-thinking test scores have been significantly modified by coaching; by explaining the scoring procedure; by offering incentives to produce a larger number of responses; by giving direct instruction; by playing games prior to testing; by exposing the subjects to comedy prior to testing; or by giving slightly different directions that provide encouragement to respond in different ways, such as suggestions to be practical and reasonable, to list as many ideas as possible, or to include as many unusual ideas as possible (Hattie, 1980; Kogan, 1983; Lissitz & Willhoft, 1985; Mayer, 1983). It appears that scores on divergent-thinking tests change very easily, but it is unlikely that actual divergent-thinking abilities improve so quickly. Put another way, divergent-thinking test scores are probably not valid for subjects who have had divergent-thinking training, even very brief training, because divergent-thinking training and divergent-thinking testing typically involve very similar kinds of tasks. (A comparable situation would be the questionable validity of an achievement or aptitude test result on a test given following training that employed questions just like the ones on the test.)

Because of their susceptibility to even the briefest interventions (which are unlikely to have caused significant real changes in general creative ability), it is difficult to interpret increases in divergent-thinking test scores following training, as in this study. Whatever validity these scores may have as measures of divergent thinking under normal conditions disappears entirely when subjects have been trained how to take the test (which is the essence, though not the intent, of most divergent-thinking training programs, including the ones used in Study 6 and in Study 7).

Wallach (1971) and Kogan (1983) admonished researchers in the field against interpreting increases in divergent-thinking test scores as evidence of actual increases in creative abilities. Even assuming that divergent thinking is a major component of creativity (under either the standard or the revised divergent-thinking theory of creativity), the validity of divergent-thinking scores of trained subjects must be questioned, as well as research results that rely upon these scores.

Therefore, the results in this study that include Torrance test scores need not be interpreted as necessarily contradicting the revised divergent-thinking theory of creativity, although they clearly offer no support. They are reported here not because they support or disprove the theory, but because (a) they relate this study to previous work, most of which has relied on divergent-thinking measures (Kogan, 1983; Torrance & Presbury, 1974), and (b) they provide a more complete picture of the outcome of these studies, which others might interpret differently.[2]

In sum, one of the two hypotheses of this study involving creative performance tests received weak support: There was a positive relationship between training in divergent thinking and both measures of creative performance. The other hypothesis—for an interpretation of those divergent-thinking training effects based on the revised divergent-thinking theory of creativity—received no support, but neither was it clearly disconfirmed. Even in the case of the positive outcome, however, the effects were minimal, and, perhaps more importantly, only two creative performance tests were employed. For these reasons, it would be premature to conclude, on the basis of this study alone, that training in divergent thinking improved creativity across performance domains (in fact, it had only a marginal, and not quite statistically significant, effect on both tests). It is also impossible to interpret these results with confidence either as the effects of improvement in general divergent-thinking skill (under the revised divergent-thinking theory of creativity) or as the effects of training in at least two (and perhaps several) different task-specific skills.

There is, finally, a very real possibility that the observed differences in Study 6 were caused by something other than training in divergent thinking, either as a general skill or as a collection of task-specific skills. It is important to note that the groups were students at different schools, and may therefore have had many other different experiences (beyond the divergent-thinking training/no divergent-think-

---

[2]There is another interesting way to consider these results that might be thought of as a modification of either the standard or the revised divergent-thinking theory. It could be that divergent thinking and creative performance have a more complex relationship than a directly linear one, such as an inverted U, in which a modest amount of the skill is better than either a small or a large amount. This is speculative, and I have performed no analyses of the data of Studies 6 and 7 to investigate what kind of relationship there might be because (a) the results of Studies 1–7 do not suggest (to me at least) sufficient evidence to warrant such an investigation, and (b) it seems too much like data snooping. I mention this possibility, however, in case others might wish to pursue it in their own research.

Howard Gruber (personal communication, September 18, 1991) made a related observation that may be closer to the truth: "A little divergent thinking might be all that is needed. Just the idea that you shouldn't fall too deeply in love with your first effort." Such a perspective fits the general idea of the revised divergent-thinking theory presented in chapter 2, in the need for a metacognitive awareness and management of divergent thinking. It also remains a viable (and yet untested) model of a general-purpose, domain-transcending skill of divergent thinking, despite (a) the results of Studies 1–5, which disconfirm the standard divergent-thinking theory of creativity, and (b) the results of Study 7, which disconfirm the revised divergent-thinking theory, at least in its linear form.

ing training difference presumed to account for the results of the study) that could have contributed to the observed differences. In terms of easily quantifiable factors, the schools are very similar (as shown in the student achievement statistics listed earlier, and the whole-school data outlined in Table 5.1). However, this was not a tightly controlled experimental study, but rather an opportunistic study that capitalized on the fact that a divergent-thinking training program had long been underway in one of the schools. Years before this study was conceived, the school that the experimental group subjects attended had decided—for reasons that must remain uncertain, but that could easily have had systemic effects that might have distorted the results of Study 6—to teach divergent thinking. In contrast, the school that the control group attended did not have any such program designed to improve students' creative-thinking skills. The fact that one school devoted time to divergent-thinking instruction might signify a different attitude toward creativity, and this attitude might have manifested itself in unknown ways to influence the creative performance of students. This is a substantial weakness, and reflects the opportunistic, nonrandom design of Study 6.

## Study 7: An Experimental Investigation*

Study 7 was an experiment designed to test the effects of training on creative performance across domains. In many ways, it was similar to Study 6, which gave weak support to the claim that training in divergent thinking improves creative performance across domains. It used subjects who were only slightly older than those in Study 6—in fact, it used many of the same subjects who were the control group for Study 6, although all training and testing occurred 6 months after the testing of Study 6. Study 7 repeated the two tasks used in Study 6 using slightly different materials. It differed from Study 6 most significantly in the level of experimental control that was possible and in the use of five rather than two tests of creativity.

There were two groups of second-grade students, each of which received equal amounts of instruction prior to testing. The groups were previously existing self-contained classes at the same school (a school in which no systematic divergent-thinking or other creativity training had been conducted). Assignment of these two groups to a condition was made randomly. The experimental group received 16 hours of training in divergent thinking over a 4-week period using a wide variety of tasks and materials, but including no direct applications of divergent thinking to tasks precisely like those later to be tested. The control group received 16 hours of practice and instruction in techniques for solving mathematical word problems over the same period. At the end of the training period, students were asked to tell stories, write poems, make collages, create mathematical word problems, and write stories. These products were evaluated for creativity by experts as in previous studies. A

---

*The principal results of Study 7 were reported, in somewhat less detail, in Baer (1992).

comparison of group means and of inter-task creativity-score correlations was made to measure the effects of the divergent-thinking training.

At the end of this section, six hypotheses of Study 7 are presented as predictions. The first five are stated from the standpoint of predicting success for the training program in improving creative performance on the various tasks. The sixth hypothesis, which was to be tested only if the first five predictions were generally confirmed, was designed to provide evidence to help decide among alternative interpretations of the success of the training. This last hypothesis is stated from the standpoint of the revised divergent-thinking theory of creativity outlined in chapter 2.

The hypotheses involving four of the tests—storytelling, story writing, poetry writing, and collage making—were straightforward: the experimental group was predicted to outperform the control group (judged by a comparison of group means). The test of creating interesting mathematical word problems, however, allowed for an interesting differential prediction. Divergent-thinking skill, when applied in creativity-relevant situations, was hypothesized to improve creativity ratings without regard to the nature of the task. It was therefore hypothesized in this study that the creativity scores of the experimental group would be elevated in all tasks over the level of performance that would be expected of an untrained group. Task-relevant knowledge, on the other hand, is widely (if not universally) believed to increase creative productivity in the particular task domain of which it is a part. (See, e.g., Amabile, 1983; Mayer, 1983; Perkins, 1981; Tardif & Sternberg, 1988.) In this study, therefore, it was hypothesized that the control group's creativity scores on the mathematical word-problem task would also be increased above the expected performance of an untrained group.

Because both groups received training (although of different types) that was expected to improve their creativity in creating mathematical word problems, it was predicted that the control group would do as well as or better than the experimental group on the word-problem task.

This is not as precise a prediction as one would like: "as well as or better than" seems to confound two predictions. Which is it to be, equal or better? Unfortunately, the sizes of the impacts of the two factors hypothesized to influence the performances of the two groups—increases in divergent-thinking skill and metacognitive awareness in one group, and increases in domain-specific knowledge in the other—are not easy to quantify. Because the control group received task-specific training on the word-problem task, as opposed to the general divergent-thinking training received by the experimental group, the effect on control-group performance on this task should, perhaps, be greater. (See Mayer, 1983, for evidence to support this contention in a similar context.) This would argue for predicting greater creative performance by the control group. But there is no formula by which these two effects can be computed relative to one another, and it was therefore difficult to make a clear prediction. For this reason the prediction for outcomes on this task was of the less precise equal-to-or-lesser-than kind. Fortunately, for the purposes of Study 7, either outcome would provide a general confirmation of the theoretical issues involved, assuming that the experimental group outperformed the control group on the other tasks. (There is also the possibility that the theory behind this differential prediction could be correct—that both kinds of training would improve performance on the word-problem-creating task—but that the effect of divergent-thinking training might be greater than the effect of the task-specific skill training. Given this possibility, a more accurate prediction might be that the experimental group would outperform the control group to a greater degree on the other tasks than on the word-problem-creating task. Fortunately, an equal-to-or-lesser-than version of this hypothesis was sufficient for the data that were observed.)

The major hypothesis tested by this study, then, was that creative performance is enhanced by training in divergent thinking, for reasons outlined earlier. This led to four predictions of more creative performance by the experimental group. A fifth prediction of equal or lesser performance by the experimental group was made based on the common belief that task-specific training improves creative performance in that domain. Because creative performance is also assumed to be influenced by other measurable skills and knowledge, tests of all of these predictions were conducted using partial correlations of residual creativity test scores (after the removal of variance attributable to reading and mathematics achievement). This analysis and the resulting group comparisons were made to assure that relevant pre-existing group differences were controlled as much as possible.

A second set of analyses was planned in the event that the group comparisons favored the experimental group (which, in fact, they did). These analyses involved correlations among the various creativity test scores, and were based on the prediction of the revised divergent-thinking theory of creativity that, for subjects trained in divergent thinking, level of skill in divergent thinking should influence creative performance in all task domains. Subjects with divergent-thinking training (the experimental group) should exhibit higher correlations among creativity test scores than subjects without such training (the control group), and total group correlations among creativity test scores should be positive. If the creativity test scores of the experimental-group subjects did not exhibit such positive correlations, alternative explanations of the effects of training, such as improvements in task-specific skills, would receive support. As with the group comparisons, residual creativity test scores were used to compute partial correlations for testing these predictions.

In summary, Study 7 was undertaken to determine if subjects trained in the general skill of divergent thinking would outperform untrained subjects in a variety of creativity-relevant tasks. If this was found to be the case, it was also a goal of this study to gather evidence to help interpret such a result (specifically if such improvement could be attributable to a general creative-thinking factor). There were six predictions, given in the following list. In each case, "trained subjects" refers to those who received divergent-thinking training, and "untrained subjects" refers to those who received training in solving mathematical word problems.

1. Trained subjects would receive higher creativity ratings than untrained subjects on the storytelling test;
2. Trained subjects would receive higher creativity ratings than untrained subjects on the story-writing test;

3. Trained subjects would receive higher creativity ratings than untrained subjects on the poetry-writing test;
4. Trained subjects would receive higher creativity ratings than untrained subjects on the collage-making test;
5. Trained subjects would not receive higher creativity ratings than untrained subjects on the word-problem-creating test; and,
6. The correlations among the creativity ratings for the total group would be positive, and correlations of the creativity ratings of trained subjects would be positive and higher than the correlations among the creativity ratings of untrained subjects, which were predicted to be zero. This final pair of predictions would be tested only if Predictions 1–4 were confirmed.

## Method

### Subjects

The subjects were the same ones described in Study 4 and used as the control group in Study 6. The present study was conducted approximately 6 months after the previous testing of these subjects, and three new students had entered one of the classes, bringing the total for the two classes to 41 students. There were 21 students in the experimental group and 20 students in the control group. According to the principal of the school, assignment of students to these two classes had been done "semi-randomly"; that is, initial assignment was made randomly by gender (to assure an approximately equal number of boys and girls in each class), and then minor adjustment had been made to balance the numbers of students receiving special education services. There were 11 girls and 9 boys in the control group, and 12 girls and 9 boys in the experimental group. California Achievement Tests were given 2 weeks prior to the beginning of the present study. The experimental group scored somewhat higher in both reading comprehension and total math (the two subtests used to partial out variance attributable to general academic skill and knowledge), but the differences were insignificant ($p > .20$) in both cases. Mean scores and standard deviations on these tests appear below in the "Pre-training" section of Table 5.5.

### Tests

There were five creative-performance tests. Two were variations of tests the same students (except for the three new students) had taken 6 months previously. Storytelling2 was the same task as the storytelling task used in Studies 4 and 6 (renamed Storytelling1 in data reported with Study 7), except that a different picture book was used (*A Boy, a Dog, a Frog, and a Friend*; Mayer & Mayer, 1971). Collage2 was the same task as the collage-making task used in Studies 4 and 6 (renamed Collage1 in data reported with Study 7), but using a somewhat different set of precut construction paper designs.

The word-problem task was the same one used in Studies 1 and 2. The poetry-writing task was the same as that used in Studies 1, 2, 3, and 5, except that subjects were free to choose the topic of their poem. They were offered "The Wind" as a possible topic, but they were not constrained as in previous studies. Pilot testing with second graders at a different school had suggested that students found it easiest to start writing with these instructions, in comparison to either topic-constrained ("Write a poem about the wind") or totally free ("Write a poem about anything that you wish") instructions. The story-writing task was the same as that used in Studies 1, 2, 3, and 5, although a different visual prompt was used. The prompt given to the students was a line drawing of two children dancing or jumping near what might be interpreted as the remains of a picnic lunch. This had been the most successful prompt (in terms of apparent ease in starting to write stories) used in pilot testing with second graders at a different school.

Following the same procedure used in Studies 4, 5, and 6, raters judged each collage, poem, or story on a 1.00–5.00 scale. There were five raters for the storytelling, story-writing, poetry, and word-problem tests, and 14 for the collage-making test. Instructions given to the raters can be found in Appendix A, and a description of the raters can be found in Appendix B. Alpha coefficient interrater reliabilities were very good, ranging from .85 to .92. All interrater reliabilities are listed in Table 5.4.

California Achievement Tests were administered by the school just prior to the beginning of Study 7 as part of the school's regular testing program.

### Procedure

The experimenter taught each class for approximately 1 hour, 4 days each week, for 4 weeks near the end of the school year. Testing took place in the two weeks immediately following the four weeks of instruction, and was also conducted by the experimenter. All instruction and testing took place in the morning. The classroom teachers were not directly involved in this instruction and testing. Some days they remained in the classroom to work at their desks, but most days they left the room to work elsewhere in the school.

The control group's instruction came exclusively from two volumes of the *Real Math* (Willoughby, Bereiter, Hilton, & Rubinstein, 1981) program. At each grade level this program includes a "Thinking Story Book" consisting of 20 extended stories involving mathematical and logical problem solving. Each of the stories is followed by a set of shorter word problems of the same kind. *Measuring Bowser* (Willoughby, Bereiter, Hilton, Rubinstein, Anderson, & Scardamalia, 1981) is the

TABLE 5.4
Interrater Reliabilities (Study 7)

| Test | Reliability Coefficient[a] | Number of Judges |
|------|------------------------|------------------|
| Storytelling2 | .85 | 5 |
| Story writing | .92 | 5 |
| Poetry | .88 | 5 |
| Word problem | .88 | 5 |
| Collage2 | .87 | 14 |

[a]Coefficient alpha (Nunnally, 1978).

second-grade level book in the "Thinking Story Book" series; *Bargains Galore* (Willoughby, Bereiter, Hilton, Rubinstein, & Scardamalia, 1981) is the third-grade level book of the series. Eight lessons from each set were used.

As an example from this set, Lesson 2 of *Bargains Galore* is "Swing Low, Sweet Willy." Willy talks his father into helping him build a backyard swing, but Willy has to plan the swing and buy all the materials himself. Students are asked along the way, as a group, to help Willy figure out how to solve problems he encounters, such as how to measure the height of the branch he plans to use for the swing. The teacher (in this case the experimenter) reads the story until there is a problem for Willy to solve, then the story is put aside temporarily as the class figures out ways to solve the problem. Many of the problems have no single right answer, as in the example given, although many others involve mathematical problem solving with quantitative answers. For example, in the problem set that follows "Swing Low, Sweet Willy," problem 6 asks, "If Willy were 12 years old, he would be twice as old as Wendy. How old is Wendy?"

The exercises used in the experimental group's training came from four sources. These are *CPS for Kids: A Resource Book for Teaching Creative Problem-Solving to Children* (Eberle & Stanish, 1980); *TAP: A Talents Unlimited Demonstration Project* (Mobile County Public Schools; 1974); *OM-AHA!: Problems to Develop Creative Thinking Skills* (Micklus, 1986); and *Project Implode* (Bella Vista Elementary School, 1965). All of the activities used were divergent-thinking training exercises, varying in length from a few minutes (in which case several were used in one class period) to an hour.

As an example of the divergent-thinking exercises, consider "Put an Alligator in the Refrigerator," from *CPS for Kids: A Resource Book for Teaching Creative Problem-Solving to Children* (Eberle, & Stanish, 1980). Students are read a scenario in which a pet alligator has become ill. The veterinarian is called, who says the alligator's temperature must be lowered quickly, and that the alligator should be put in the refrigerator to accomplish this. The task is to think of as many ways as possible to put an alligator into a refrigerator. Students work on this as a group. A second task is to think of a name for the alligator that no one else in the class would think of, which is later to be shared with the group. The directions encourage students to think of as many solutions as possible, and to come up with the most unusual names they can imagine.

An activity called "Hats" from *Project Implode* (Bella Vista Elementary School, 1965, p. 20) starts with a discussion of the many kinds of hats people wear. Then, students are asked to stretch their imaginations and think of as many uses as they can for hats. Students individually write as many uses as they can think of for 5 minutes, then share their lists with the class to make a master list.

"Stocking Stuffin'" is an activity from *TAP: A Talents Unlimited Demonstration Project* (Mobile County Public Schools; 1974, p. 17). Students are told that Santa Claus might be lonely (and overworked!) making his Christmas visits alone, and the class is invited to think of unusual companions Santa might take with him in the sleigh to keep him company. After a few minutes of brainstorming, students are given a sheet of paper with line drawings of six stockings and asked to think of unusual surprises that could be found in a Christmas stocking. Students are asked to fill the stockings by drawing these surprises coming out of the stockings.

One of the activities from *OM-AHA!: Problems to Develop Creative Thinking Skills* (Micklus, 1986, p. 60) is "Catch a Mouse." Students brainstorm as many ways as possible that one might catch a mouse or remove it from a house.

Brainstorming rules apply in all these exercises: That is, the goal is to produce a large quantity of ideas, not (necessarily) ideas of high quality; there is to be no judgement of ideas as good or bad; unusual ideas are welcome; and adapting or modifying previously suggested ideas is encouraged. The general direction used was to "think of many, varied, unusual ideas for [whatever the problem was]."

The tests were not identified as tests; however, students were instructed to work alone, and to write their answers on paper rather than report them orally (except for the storytelling and collage-making tasks, described later). The students in the experimental group were not explicitly instructed to use divergent thinking—to do so would have required different instructions for the experimental and control groups—but the presence of the experimenter, who had been teaching the students divergent thinking for 4 weeks, was probably a salient clue that the use of divergent thinking would be appropriate. Students were told that if they needed help with spelling a word to raise their hand and the experimenter would come to them and write it out for them on scrap paper. This had been a standard procedure in both classes all year, except that, generally, the students came to the teachers' desks rather than vice versa. The experimenter typed all stories, poems, and word problems before sending them to raters, who worked independently of one another.

The collage-making task was conducted by the experimenter as an art class. The task was familiar, as all but three of the experimental group students had done the same collage-making task 6 months previously, and the students were very familiar with collage making. There were several changes in the assortment of 100-plus construction paper cut-out designs from the set provided at the previous testing, but otherwise the task was the same. All subjects received identical sets of materials, of course, including their own container of school glue.

The previous collage-making test had been administered individually to make it impossible for students to copy ideas from one another, but a different problem was encountered: Some students, probably shy or merely uncomfortable working alone in a room with the experimenter, rushed to finish as quickly as possible. Students appeared very comfortable working on the collages in their classrooms; they were accustomed to doing artwork this way, and they could at most see the work of three or four other students. Casual observation suggested little copying, although there was no direct control or measure of this. Amabile's (1982, 1983) validation of collage making as a test of creative performance used similar group administrations.

Each judge viewed all the collages at the same time. Judges worked independently of one another without conferring or learning of one another's ratings. The collages were displayed in random order on several large art tables, and judges walked among them and rated them in any order they wished.

The storytelling task was conducted, typed, and rated as in Study 4. The

TABLE 5.5
Mean Test Scores (Study 7 and Study 4)

| Test | Total Group | Control | Experimental | F | df |
|------|-------------|---------|--------------|---|-----|
| Pre-training | | | | | |
| Reading | 74.6 (41) | 70.6 (20) | 78.4 (21) | 1.66 | (1,40) |
| achievement[a] | [19.5] | [21.3] | [17.3] | | |
| Math | 67.4 (41) | 64.7 (20) | 69.9 (21) | .65 | (1,40) |
| achievement[b] | [20.6] | [22.3] | [19.0] | | |
| Storytelling1[c] | 2.63 (36) | 2.57 (19) | 2.71 (17) | .27 | (1,35) |
| | [.83] | [.77] | [.84] | | |
| Collage1[c] | 2.71 (38) | 2.94 (20) | 2.46 (18) | 3.74* | (1,37) |
| | [.81] | [.75] | [.78] | | |
| Post-training | | | | | |
| Storytelling2[c] | 3.13 (40) | 2.86 (20) | 3.40 (20) | 4.55** | (1,39) |
| | [.83] | [.77] | [.82] | | |
| Story writing[c] | 2.78 (41) | 2.35 (20) | 3.20 (21) | 9.50*** | (1,40) |
| | [.98] | [.99] | [.77] | | |
| Poetry[c] | 2.69 (39) | 2.16 (20) | 3.26 (19) | 15.32*** | (1,38) |
| | [1.04] | [.98] | [.77] | | |
| Word problem[c] | 2.93 (41) | 3.04 (20) | 2.82 (21) | .69 | (1,40) |
| | [.85] | [.97] | [.74] | | |
| Collage2[c] | 3.04 (41) | 2.96 (20) | 3.12 (21) | .54 | (1,40) |
| | [.66] | [.55] | [.76] | | |

*Note.* $n$ of each group appears in parentheses following the mean score. Standard deviations appear in brackets beneath scores.

[a]Percentile scores, California Achievement Test (reading comprehension).

[b]Percentile scores, California Achievement Test (total math).

[c]1.00–5.00 scale

*$p < .10$ two-tailed. **$p < .05$ two-tailed. ***$p < .01$ two-tailed.

All other comparisons $p > .20$ two-tailed.

poetry-writing, story-writing, and word-problem-creating tasks were conducted and typed as in Studies 1–3, but the 1.00–5.00 rating scaled adopted for all tests beginning with Study 4 was employed.

The group tests were administered on four consecutive days; the storytelling test was given individually the following week. There were no time limits imposed on the students, but none took more than 1 hour to complete any one of the tests. Perhaps students were accustomed to the experimenter's being there for 1 hour and paced themselves accordingly; whatever the reason, none of the students appeared to be rushed and none complained that they needed more time. Many students finished in less than 1 hour, and these students were invited to read quietly while their classmates continued working on the assigned task. This, too, was standard procedure in both classes.

Students who were absent the day of testing were not retested, as it was felt that their performance could not be validly compared to that of students who had not learned of the task in advance. This affected only one of the tests, the poetry-writing task: Two students in the experimental group did not write poems. All students completed the storytelling task, but the voice of one student in the experimental group was too soft to be understood on tape. Numbers of subjects in each condition for each task appear in Table 5.5. Samples of subject's stories, poems, and word problems are presented in Appendix C.

## Results

The divergent-thinking group had higher creativity scores on the four tests for which this difference had been predicted, although only three of those differences were statistically significant: storytelling, $F(1, 39) = 4.55, p < .05$; story-writing, $F(1, 40) = 9.50, p < .01$; and poetry-writing $F(1, 38) = 15.32, p < .01$ (two-tailed tests). These results are summarized in Table 5.5.

Regression equations were used to partial out variance attributable to reading achievement and mathematics achievement, as measured by the California Achievement Tests. Total variance accounted for by reading and mathematics achievement was significant for the story-writing test ($R^2 = .29$, adjusted $R^2 = .25$, $p < .01$) and the storytelling test ($R^2 = .20$, adjusted $R^2 = .16, p < .05$). Creativity test variance attributable to achievement test scores is listed in Table 5.6.

Between-group comparisons using residual creativity test scores (with variance attributable to reading and mathematics achievement test scores removed) followed exactly the same pattern as the raw score comparisons, with the divergent-thinking group scoring significantly higher on the same three tasks: storytelling, $F(1, 39) = 4.19, p < .05$; story-writing, $F(1, 40) = 7.70, p < .01$; and poetry-writing $F(1, 38) = 13.28, p < .01$. These mean residual test scores are listed in Table 5.7.

A re-analysis of the results of previous testing of the 38 students (reported in Studies 4 and 6) who had taken part in the earlier experiment was conducted to see if the difference in storytelling creativity could be attributed to differences that preceded training. Differences between the scores of the two groups on pre-training

TABLE 5.6
Creativity Test Score Variance Accounted for by Reading and Math Achievement Scores (Study 7 and Study 4)

| Test | $R^2$ | Adjusted $R^2$ |
|---|---|---|
| Study 7 | | |
| Storytelling2 | .20* | .16 |
| Story writing | .29** | .25 |
| Poetry | .04 | − .02 |
| Word problem | .09 | .04 |
| Collage2 | .00 | − .05 |
| Study 4 | | |
| Storytelling1 | .06 | .00 |
| Collage1 | .01 | − .05 |
| Torrance test | .20* | .16 |

$*p < .05$ two-tailed. $**p < .01$ two-tailed.

TABLE 5.7
Comparison of Mean Residual Test Scores (Study 7 and Study 4)

| Test | Control | Experimental | F | df |
|------|---------|--------------|---|-----|
| Post-training | | | | |
| Storytelling2 | 2.90 | 3.367 | 4.19** | (1,39) |
| Story writing | 2.44 | 3.10 | 7.70*** | (1,40) |
| Poetry | 2.19 | 3.22 | 13.28*** | (1,38) |
| Word problem | 3.10 | 2.77 | 1.64 | (1,40) |
| Collage2 | 2.97 | 3.11 | .47 | (1,41) |
| Pre-training | | | | |
| Storytelling1 | 2.60 | 2.67 | .04 | (1,35) |
| Collage1 | 2.92 | 2.47 | 3.29* | (1,37) |

*Note.* Variance attributable to reading and math achievement test scores has been removed. All scores were computed as deviation scores and then added to the original total group mean.
*$p < .10$ two-tailed. **$p < .05$ two-tailed. ***$p < .01$ two-tailed.
All other comparisons $p > .20$ two-tailed.

TABLE 5.8
Zero-Order Correlations Among Creativity Tests (Total Group, Study 7)

| Test | Storytelling2 | Story Writing | Poetry | Word Problem | Collage2 |
|------|---------------|---------------|--------|--------------|----------|
| Storytelling2 | 1.00 | .46* | .25 | −.11 | .09 |
| Story writing | | 1.00 | .31 | −.12 | .04 |
| Poetry | | | 1.00 | −.03 | .26 |
| Word problem | | | | 1.00 | .02 |
| Collage2 | | | | | 1.00 |

*$p < .01$ two-tailed.

storytelling creativity (Storytelling1), both before and after variance attributable to reading and mathematics achievement had been partialled out, were negligible. The control group scored higher on collage making (Collage1, $p < .10$). These results are included in Tables 5.5 and 5.7 in the "Pre-training" sections.

Because training in divergent thinking had produced a significant difference on three of the four tasks for which such a difference had been predicted, an analysis was made of the correlations among creativity test scores. Tables 5.8, 5.9, and 5.10 report zero-order correlations of test scores for the total group, control group, and experimental group, respectively. For the total group, only the story-writing/storytelling correlation was significant ($r = .46$, $p < .01$), although there were more positive than negative correlations. The three tasks that might most appropriately be described as verbal tasks—poetry-writing, story-writing, and storytelling—produced three of the largest correlations.

For the control group, the storytelling/story-writing correlation was the same as for the total group, although because of the smaller $n$ the significance level was less extreme ($r = .46$, $p < .05$). Although some of the remaining correlations approached significance, they were a mixture of positive and negative correlations with no obvious pattern.

For the experimental group, 8 of the 10 correlations were positive, but none reached even the .10 level of significance. Taken alone, these experimental group results suggest correlations of the kind predicted by the revised theory, although very modest ones lacking statistical significance. However, the creativity test scores used to compute these correlation coefficients include the effects of the kinds of reading and mathematics skills assessed on standardized achievement tests. These skills both (a) preceded training (standardized testing happened 2 weeks prior to the beginning of Study 7), and (b) are not the kind of general creativity-relevant skills being sought—skills that take one *beyond* the level of correct, skillful performance to that of creative performance. Of greater interest to this analysis, therefore, are the partial correlations among creativity test scores (with variance attributable to reading and mathematics achievement removed). These are reported in Tables 5.11, 5.12, and 5.13.

TABLE 5.9
Zero-Order Correlations Among Creativity Tests (Control Group, Study 7)

| Test | Storytelling2 | Story Writing | Poetry | Word Problem | Collage2 |
|------|------|------|------|------|------|
| Storytelling2 | 1.00 | .46** | .10 | − .42* | − .02 |
| Story writing | | 1.00 | .01 | − .25 | − .35 |
| Poetry | | | 1.00 | .01 | .39* |
| Word problem | | | | 1.00 | .09 |
| Collage2 | | | | | 1.00 |

*$p < .10$. **$p < .05$ two-tailed.

TABLE 5.10
Zero-Order Correlations Among Creativity Tests (Experimental Group, Study 7)

| Test | Storytelling2 | Story Writing | Poetry | Word Problem | Collage2 |
|------|------|------|------|------|------|
| Storytelling2 | 1.00 | .26 | .13 | .34 | .07 |
| Story writing | | 1.00 | .16 | .22 | .29 |
| Poetry | | | 1.00 | .10 | − .02 |
| Word problem | | | | 1.00 | − .01 |
| Collage2 | | | | | 1.00 |

TABLE 5.11
Partial Correlations Among Creativity Tests[a] (Total Group, Study 7)

| Test | Storytelling2 | Story Writing | Poetry | Word Problem | Collage2 |
|------|------|------|------|------|------|
| Storytelling2 | 1.00 | .38** | .30* | − .22 | .11 |
| Story writing | | 1.00 | .31* | − .35** | .03 |
| Poetry | | | 1.00 | − .07 | .24 |
| Word problem | | | | 1.00 | .01 |
| Collage2 | | | | | 1.00 |

[a]Correlations of residual scores after variance attributable to standardized test scores (reading achievement and math achievement) have been removed.

*$p < .10$ two-tailed. **$p < .05$ two-tailed.

TABLE 5.12
Partial Correlations Among Creativity Tests[a] (Control Group, Study 7)

| Test | Storytelling2 | Story Writing | Poetry | Word Problem | Collage2 |
|------|---------------|---------------|--------|--------------|----------|
| Storytelling2 | 1.00 | .53** | .21 | − .37 | .18 |
| Story writing | | 1.00 | .12 | − .43* | − .04 |
| Poetry | | | 1.00 | .04 | .45** |
| Word problem | | | | 1.00 | .25 |
| Collage2 | | | | | 1.00 |

[a]Correlations of residual scores after variance attributable to standardized test scores (reading achievement and math achievement) have been removed.
*$p < .10$ two-tailed. **$p < .05$ two-tailed.

TABLE 5.13
Partial Correlations Among Creativity Tests[a] (Experimental Group, Study 7)

| Test | Storytelling2 | Story Writing | Poetry | Word Problem | Collage2 |
|------|---------------|---------------|--------|--------------|----------|
| Storytelling2 | 1.00 | − .20 | .13 | .19 | − .05 |
| Story writing | | 1.00 | .10 | − .05 | .01 |
| Poetry | | | 1.00 | .04 | − .11 |
| Word problem | | | | 1.00 | − .18 |
| Collage2 | | | | | 1.00 |

[a]Correlations of residual scores after variance attributable to standardized test scores (verbal IQ, reading achievement, math IQ, math achievement) have been removed.

For the total group, two partial correlations were significant at the .05 level. One was positive: storytelling/story writing, $r = .38$. The other was negative: story writing/word problem, $r = -.35$. The poetry/story-writing ($r = .31$) and poetry/storytelling ($r = .30$) partial correlations approached significance ($p < .10$).

The pattern of partial correlations in the control group was similar to that of the total group, but some of the partial correlations (both positive and negative) were higher. The highest correlation coefficient—storytelling/story writing, $r = .53$, $p < .05$—accounted for over 25% of the remaining variance. Seven of the partial correlations were positive, and three were negative.

The partial correlations for the experimental group are shown in Table 5.13. There were 10 correlations among the five creativity tests. They were scattered in what appears to be a random pattern centered around zero. Five were positive and five were negative; none approached significance (even the largest correlation coefficient in the set had a $p$ value greater than .35); and none accounted for more than 4% of the total variance of the two tests involved. This is similar to the kind of results found in previous experiments involving subjects untrained in divergent thinking (as described in Studies 1–5), and, in fact, shows even less evidence of a single factor influencing creativity than was found in the control group.

## Discussion

The results of Study 7 suggest that, although training in divergent thinking influences creativity on a variety of tasks, these effects are not due to a single factor such as general divergent-thinking skill. On three tests—poetry writing, story writing, and storytelling—the group trained in divergent thinking scored higher than the control group by a considerable (and statistically significant) margin; therefore, Predictions 1, 2, and 3 were confirmed. This represents a significant change as a result of just 16 hours of training, an impressive confirmation of the value of creativity training using divergent-thinking exercises. However, the essentially random pattern of partial correlations (with variance attributable to reading and mathematics achievement removed) among these tests for both the total group and the experimental group followed the same pattern observed previously with untrained groups, suggesting that many factors, rather than one, were involved in the success of the training.

Interpretation of the results of the collage-making and word-problem-creating tests is less straightforward, although not in ways that cast doubt on the overall interpretation of the pattern of results. On the word-problem-creating test, the divergent-thinking group scored slightly lower than the control group, confirming Prediction 5. The control group had received 4 weeks of training in solving problems such as those subjects were asked to write. Although there is no way to directly assess the impact of this training on subjects' creativity in writing mathematical word problems, it is likely that greater skill in solving such problems would facilitate the creation of interesting new problems. This is, in fact, one of the primary reasons that this kind of training was provided for the control group. The fact that the divergent-thinking group did only slightly less well than the control group suggests that the divergent-thinking training may have also had a positive impact on creativity in this task; however, the data do not tell us whether (a) both groups' scores on this test were improved by training, with the control group receiving a slighter greater impact; (b) both groups' scores on this test were improved by training to an equal degree; (c) only the experimental group's scores on this test were improved by training, and only slightly; or (d) neither group's scores on this test were affected by training. The results *do* suggest, however, that something different was happening on this test than what happened on the other tests.

The divergent-thinking group did slightly better than the control group on the collage-making task, reversing a somewhat poorer performance than the control group on this task in testing 6 months prior to training. Thus, divergent-thinking training may have also had an impact, although a smaller one, on this test. To test this, an additional regression analysis was conducted in which pre-training differences in collage-making ratings were partialled out before comparing the groups, but the difference, although larger, still fell short of statistical significance. Because not all subjects had taken part in Study 6, only 37 subjects could be included in this comparison; $F(36, 1) = .98$, $p > .10$. Therefore, although the evidence pointed in the predicted direction, Prediction 4 was not confirmed.

The tests on which the most significant differences between the two groups were found—the poetry-writing, story-writing, and storytelling tasks —are tasks that are largely verbal in nature. This was not due to any explicit training in verbal skills. Both groups received training that was highly interactive and verbal, with approximately equal amounts of time in the two groups devoted to large-group discussion, small-group discussion, and individual written activities. Despite these correspondences in the amounts of time spent in various kinds of verbal activities, the divergent-thinking training influenced creative performance in ways that the training in solving word problems did not. It is important to emphasize that the effects of the divergent-thinking training, although concentrated to some extent in what might be termed the *verbal domain*, were not attributable to a single verbal factor, because creativity scores on those tasks were not correlated with one another for the experimental group. Therefore, Prediction 6 was disconfirmed.

Although, as a result of this and previous studies, divergent thinking does not appear to be either a single skill or a distinct set of skills widely applicable within broad cognitive domains (such as those proposed by Gardner, 1983, 1988), what is commonly referred to as divergent thinking may nonetheless describe a large constellation of skills, each influencing creative performance on different tasks. It is apparent that changes in creative performance can be achieved using training materials that tap these skills. Unfortunately, this study cannot determine the nature of such skills, nor speak to what kinds of training led to which effects; it can only claim that no single factor was found to influence the creative performance of trained subjects in different domains.

Study 7 adds to the evidence that single-factor theories of creativity are inadequate, whether the single factor is divergent thinking or some other broadly applicable skill or trait. Even theories that include several different kinds of divergent thinking are not compatible with the results of this study or those reported earlier. Nor does a theory in which divergent-thinking competence and performance are separated—with divergent thinking having an effect only among those who have learned how and when to apply it, as in the revised divergent-thinking theory proposed in chapter 2—fit the evidence gathered in Study 7.

A distinction must be made, however, between theories of divergent thinking and creativity-training programs based on those theories. Study 7 supports claims made by such programs that they can improve creative performance across task domains. This may have to do with practicing a variety of skills, as suggested above, although the exact nature of those skills, and the mechanisms by which they influence creative performance, remain unknown.

# 6

# Conclusions

## SUMMARY OF THE EVIDENCE

The search for general, domain-transcending creative-thinking skills has led to a curious conclusion. Although all theories of creativity centering on a single factor (including specifically the revised divergent-thinking theory proposed in chapter 2) have been tested and found wanting, one of those theories—the divergent-thinking theory—has been found to be the source of a successful approach to teaching creative thinking. There is, one might initially conclude on the basis of the correlational research reported in chapters 4 and 5, little reason to retain the divergent-thinking theory (or any general theory) of creativity, and yet some of divergent thinking's offspring—in the form of a variety of creativity-training programs and exercises based on divergent-thinking theory—appear to be worth both saving and examining further.

To summarize the course of the investigations reported in chapters 4 and 5: A series of experiments designed to test for the existence of any general creativity-relevant factor suggested that no such factor exists, at least for subjects without special training. A revision of the most influential theory of creativity, the divergent-thinking theory, was attempted, in part because of the frequently reported success of divergent-thinking training in enhancing creativity in many domains. This revised theory could have accounted for both (a) the failure of divergent thinking to influence the creative performance of subjects untrained in divergent-thinking techniques, and (b) the positive effects of divergent-thinking training on creative performance. A preliminary study (Study 6) provided some weak evidence in support of the revised theory, although because this study was small in scope (only two creative-performance measures were employed) and methodologically flawed in several respects, it would have required replication even if it had yielded more significant outcomes. A more carefully controlled experiment employing five creative-performance tests was conducted to test for the effects of divergent-thinking training on creative performance, and this experiment (Study 7) provided ample evidence that the subjects trained in divergent thinking were more creative on a variety of tasks than the untrained subjects. However, an analysis of those effects revealed that the group differences could not be explained by any single factor.

It should be added that the pattern of results of Study 7, as well as the results of the previous studies, cannot be explained by any heretofore proposed division of divergent thinking into a discrete set of divergent-thinking skills. Guilford (1967) grouped divergent-production factors (of which he theorized there would be 24, although he identified only 16) into four categories: fluency, flexibility, originality, and elaboration. Later theorists tended to use these same four groupings (Kogan, 1983; Torrance, 1990; Wallach, 1970). Such divisions do not change the conclusion that divergent-thinking theories are inadequate, however. None of these theories argues, for example, that fluency would be more important in writing poetry, whereas elaboration would aid in storytelling. Even when divergent thinking is divided into four separate divergent-thinking factors, each factor is theorized to be generally applicable across all possible task domains. (Such a division, it should also be noted, is one that factor-analytic studies of the results of divergent-thinking test scores do not support; see Borland, 1986; Heausler & Thompson, 1988; Hocevar, 1979; Kogan, 1983; Runco, 1986a). Therefore, the failure of a general creativity-relevant factor to emerge is as crippling to a divergent-thinking theory that posits distinct divergent-thinking skills as it is to a theory of a single divergent-thinking skill. Runco's (1990) suggestion that ideational/divergent thinking may be domain-specific in the manner of Gardner's (1983) "intelligences" is also contradicted by the results reported in chapters 4 and 5, although this is certainly a step in the right direction. The next step that needs to be taken is to consider task-specific, rather than broad domain-specific, versions of divergent-thinking skills.

Studies 1–5 provided evidence that general, domain-independent factors (such as divergent-thinking) do not influence creative performance across a variety of tasks. The wide age range of the subjects taking part in these studies (ages 7–40) allows fairly broad generalization of those findings. Study 7 provided evidence that such general factors do not influence creative performance even among subjects trained in divergent thinking; however, only second-grade subjects took part in this study. It is therefore possible that the results would be different with subjects of different ages. Based on (a) the parallel results among untrained subjects in Studies 1–5, and (b) the general trend in cognitive development toward increased, rather than decreased, differentiation of functions, this seems unlikely. However, one might expect to find greater ability among older subjects to apply metacognitive strategies—in this case, to know when to use divergent-thinking skills—that could result in a greater impact among older subjects of training in divergent thinking. This, in turn, could result in the emergence of a general creativity-relevant factor related to divergent thinking. A replication of Study 7 with older subjects would help to resolve this question.

It must be noted that the kind of creative performance being investigated in these studies is only one kind of creative performance, and there are other kinds of creative performance to which these results cannot be generalized. One important caveat is that the subjects in these studies were not identified as highly creative in any field of endeavor. As has been often noted (e.g., Bamberger, 1990; Gruber &

Davis, 1988; Johnson-Laird, 1988b; Tardif & Sternberg, 1988), expert-level creativity may involve very different processes than the more "garden-variety" creativity under consideration in all the research reported earlier. However, it is unlikely that expert-level creativity operates in a domain-independent way. Studies of genius, such as those conducted by Gruber and his students (e.g., Gruber, 1981; Gruber & Davis, 1988; Jeffrey, 1983), typically assert extreme domain dependence for the creativity of their subjects. Nonetheless, the studies reported here, although suggesting a similarity between these two very different kinds of creative performance, cannot speak directly to the issue of domain or task limitations at the level of creative genius.

A second caveat is that people may (and in some ways certainly do) act differently when they are not acting as subjects of experiments (or as students in school, which was the setting for all the studies). Naturalistic studies that would parallel the studies reported earlier may be difficult to design and run, but without such evidence, caution must be exercised in generalizing the results of these studies to creative performance apart from school or testing settings. Although this may seem at first to be a major limitation, the school- and test-like settings of these studies are not radically different from the constraints under which much creative behavior takes place, especially the garden-variety, everyday kinds of creativity about which these studies are concerned. For many of the more obvious applications to which these results might be put—in education generally, and in creativity training in particular—there is little problem of over-generalization due to differences in settings. There may, of course, be general, domain-independent, creativity-relevant thinking skills at work in nonschool and nontest-like settings. But even if such general creative-thinking skills do exist, it is reasonable to assume that divergent thinking (by which I mean here a unified, domain-transcending skill or set of skills) is not such a skill, because if divergent thinking does not play a significant role even in creative performance in settings where it is highly cued, as was the case in the Study 7, it seems unlikely that it will be found to be an important factor in settings where divergent thinking is less salient.

It is important to emphasize that the divergent-thinking training did have a significant impact on subjects' creative performance on several tasks, even though this does not appear to have resulted from an increased proficiency in a single skill. There are, it would appear, a number of different skills being practiced through the use of divergent-thinking exercises, skills that may be especially relevant to creative performance on verbal tasks. For example, exercises in which subjects are asked to find words that meet particular constraints, such as words beginning with a particular sound, might be predicted to increase poetry-writing creativity. It seems reasonable to predict that inroads into both understanding creativity and improving training in creativity will most likely be found using fairly task-specific, limited-range skills and training (such as the example just given involving what might be considered training in the skill of alliteration). Training in creativity will probably be found to be most effective when targeted narrowly at improving creative performance in specific task domains.

No finding is final; no question can be ruled settled for all time; and no pattern of results can us assure that new experiments will never cause us to doubt our conclusions. However, the more research evidence we can point to, the more frequently those experiments are replicated, and the more diverse the indicators that all point in the same direction, the greater confidence we can have in our conclusions. The search reported earlier for general factors influencing creative performance, as well as the effort to revise (and thereby revive) the most widely followed general theory of creativity (the divergent-thinking theory), point in the same direction: away from a divergent-thinking theory, or from any single-factor theory, of the cognitive mechanisms underlying creativity. Further research with different tasks and different age groups could help clarify this conclusion (or, possibly, cause us to rethink it). A more productive area for future research might be to attempt to isolate which kinds of divergent-thinking training lead to enhanced creative performance in particular tasks. It may be, for example, that what is useful is the particular content that is used in training. That is, the more similar the content used in training to the content of the task used as a test, the greater the influence on creative performance. There may also be certain kinds of cognitive tasks, such as listing possible uses for some object (a common divergent-thinking exercise), that influence certain kinds of task performance. Such research could improve both (a) our understanding of the kinds of knowledge and cognitive processes important in different kinds of creative thinking, and (b) our ability to target training to the kinds of tasks that matter to us.

## A MULTILEVEL FRAMEWORK FOR THINKING ABOUT CREATIVITY

The research results reported in chapters 4 and 5, as well as the analyses of previous research findings presented in chapters 2 and 3, make what I believe is a strong case for a task-specific approach to thinking about creativity. The divergent-thinking theory of creativity, which has been the most successful general theory of creativity, has, because of its prominence, been most directly attacked. However, the evidence is equally damning of any general theory of creativity.

Sternberg (1990) argued that different "metaphors of mind" guide the kinds of theories of intelligence psychologists construct. Different metaphors suggest different questions and different theories, and a major source of disagreement comes from the fact that theorists working in different camps are simply not trying to answer the same questions. For example, much of the work in intelligence testing has been based on what Sternberg terms a *geographic* metaphor, in which the goal has been to construct a "map" of the mind. The theories (and tests) that have been produced to answer the questions raised by the geographic metaphor provide a somewhat static picture of the nature of intelligence, which fits the geographic or map-making metaphor well. In contrast, theorists using the *computational* metaphor—perhaps the most prominent model in cognitive psychology today—tend to emphasize the processes of cognition; those who subscribe to the *biological* metaphor try to understand intelligence in terms of the functioning of the brain;

and so on, with each metaphor raising different issues and questions, which naturally result in very different sets of theories and answers. (The other metaphors for ways of thinking about intelligence that Sternberg offers are the *epistemological, anthropological, sociological,* and *systems.*)

Different metaphors lead to different questions (and different answers), and the theories deriving from the different metaphors provide different glimpses of the "true" nature of intelligence. Sternberg argued that theories based on different metaphors can provide one another important insights, and theories arising from diverse approaches might, in some cases, be profitably combined to build more inclusive theories. Theories that spring from different metaphors do not provide competing answers to the same questions, however, and they cannot therefore be fruitfully compared or set against one another as a test of their adequacy. One might debate which is the most appropriate metaphor (or the most important set of questions), and indeed there have been many arguments that can be reduced to disputes over which metaphor(s), and which sets of questions, are most important. But each vantage point provides its own insight, and generates its own partial theory, of the nature of intelligence.

I believe that a similar situation exists—or should exist—in creativity theory. That is, different theories need to exist for different purposes, driven by different sets of questions (if not by explicit metaphors). As I suggested earlier, there may be an important role for domain-transcending, universal theories of creativity (such as divergent-thinking theories) high up in a hierarchy of creativity theories—even though, at the operational (or computational) level, we know that the skills such a high-level theory groups together are actually separate, discrete, nongeneralizable skills.

One such role is as a source of hypotheses for task-specific creativity-relevant skills. For example, although it seems clear that fluency, as a general cognitive mechanism, is not psychologically "real," at least as a general creativity-relevant skill, it is very possible that many task-specific subdivisions of what is generally thought of as the general skill of fluency are important in creative performance in different task domains. It may be that there is a skill such as "fluency in generating many rhyming words" that influences poetry-writing creativity (although I must point out that I have no evidence of this—this is a question in the realm of matching specific skills to creative performance on specific tasks, a large research arena in which I believe some of the most important future research in creativity will occur). Similarly, it may be that there are skills such as "fluency in producing many words that begin with the same sound" and "fluency in inventing many metaphors for a given concept"—two more hypothetical skills that might contribute to poetry-writing creativity. Assuming, for the moment, that these three fluency-related skills exist, the three may themselves be related—that is, they may share some cognitive operations, or for some other reason tend to co-occur—or they may be entirely discrete, unrelated skills. Moving from the writing of poetry to other creativity-relevant task domains, there might be different fluency-related skills—"fluency at generating many different configurations with a given set of shapes" and "fluency in producing many different number combinations equal to a given number," for example, to suggest two that might be related to some of the tasks used in the experiments in chapters 4 and 5. These, in turn, might be totally discrete skills, or they might be related to some other fluency-related skills.

Further subdivisions are always possible, of course. "Fluency in generating many rhyming words" might be comprised of many discrete subskills that could be identified through careful research. On the other hand, it is entirely possible that there are no distinguishable subskills and that this is as far down as this kind of analysis can be pushed (in which case "fluency in generating many rhyming words" would be the lowest level construct related to this skill that is available to an information-processing account—although in such a case, this lowest level construct would quite possibly be an output function of a subsymbolic, lower level, connectionist network). The important point is that different levels of analysis, like different metaphors, propose and answer different questions. This leads to a second important role of universal, domain-transcending theories of creativity: convenience in thinking about creativity as a broad psychological concept, however irrelevant that concept might be at the level of cognitive processes. (In an interesting way this follows Whitehead's advice that we should "seek generalizations and distrust them" [quoted by Lee Schulman in an interview with Ron Brandt; Brandt, 1992, p. 19].)

There is, it should be noted, a more radical possibility regarding the highest level at which one can appropriately pitch a theory of the cognitive mechanisms underlying a particular kind of creative performance. If the strongest possible version of the eliminative connectionist story tells the whole story of the architecture of cognition, then there are no intermediate levels of meaning, skills, or representations to be identified in our efforts to understand the cognitive-processing mechanisms underlying creative performance. In such a scenario, it would also appear to be the case, based on the results of Studies 1–7, that very little generalization occurs across tasks in such a network, at least as far as creativity-relevant cognitive mechanisms are concerned. Although outputs relevant to creative performance in diverse domains would be computed on the same connectionist network of hidden units and weighted connection strengths, each task domain might nonetheless have a distinct arrangement of input–output relationships.

This is, curiously, rather like a connectionist version of Mednick's (1962) steep associative hierarchy (discussed in chapter 2), except that in the connectionist case it would probably be pretty much equally characteristic of the performance of all individuals, not a variable on which individuals showed reliable (according to Mednick) differences, and the associations would be between task domains, not concepts. That such discrimination of seemingly similar functions is possible on a connectionist network—although in a task domain dealing with much lower level, routine, and noncreative kinds of tasks—is demonstrated in the success of connectionist networks to produce correct past-tense forms of irregular verbs. A single network of hidden units and adjustable connections strengths can learn, by adjusting the weights of the same array of connections based on feedback, all the different irregular-verb past-tense forms in English, and the network can continue to match past-tense verb forms reliably to their present-tense forms even as new learning continues to occur across the system. It should be recalled that each such memory is distributed throughout the network, not localized in any one part of the system. No present tense/past tense pairs are directly stored, as such, anywhere in the network, and the network of connection strengths that has learned these pairs continues to change as it learns new associations—and yet, the correct relationships between previously learned present-tense inputs and past-tense outputs can be maintained. Interestingly, the very same network that produces unique past-tense forms for irregular English verbs is also able to produce correct regular past-tense verb forms in what appears (to an observer unaware of how the network computes its output) to follow rule-like functions, although there are no rules, algorithms, or heuristics of any kind encoded, as such, anywhere in the network (Pinker & A. Prince, 1987; Rumelhart & McClelland, 1986a).

It may be, however—as some theorists working within the connectionist camp have argued (e.g., Miikkulainen & Dyer, 1991; Minsky, 1986; Norman, 1986)—that although the foundational architecture of cognition is best described using connectionist models, higher level cognitive processes are constructed from the coordinated actions of several interacting lower level connectionist modules. There are many possible versions of such a weak connectionist approach, with the weakest and most trivial scenario being one in which (a) connectionism is simply a way to instantiate symbolic processing, (b) the computer hardware–software metaphor for the distinction between brains and cognition remains unscathed, and (c) standard information-processing models of cognition are entirely unaffected. At the opposite end of this continuum, of course, is eliminative connectionism. The infinite number of possible in-between positions vary on at least three dimensions: (a) the level at which higher level symbolic processing "takes over" from lower level connectionist modules, (b) the number of distinguishable levels involved in higher level processing, and (c) the range or general applicability of the higher level processors employed at each level.

In the case of creative-thinking skills, it would appear that at whatever level symbolic, rule-based information processing begins, the processing mechanisms that lead to creative performance are very task specific. Symbolic processing might emerge only at the very end of the line (or perhaps I should say "at the output end of the network," because it would clearly not be a one-step-at-a-time serial process), when the outputs of one or more connectionist modules are translated into the actions that produce the movements, symbols, or artifacts that, in turn, constitute the sculpture, dance, poem, theory, score of music, or whatever other product is created. Under weaker connectionist scenarios, however, identifiable task-specific skills would emerge much earlier in the creative process.

A strong version of connectionism, then, leaves little about which to theorize other than the overall wiring of the network (which is no trivial problem, by any means). If eliminative connectionism is the true story, then the work to be done in understanding creativity is more in the manner of building simulations than theories, and then matching the inputs and outputs of such simulations to those of human subjects to see if there is a correspondence that would at least demonstrate that the simulation was a possible model for human creative performance. But if symbolic processing, at whatever level, takes over to coordinate and make use of the outputs of lower level connectionist modules, then a major goal of creativity theory and experimentation is to identify the task-specific skills that underlie creative performance in diverse task domains.

It seems clear (from the results of Studies 1–7) that the cognitive-processing mechanisms of interest to creativity researchers should not be general, domain-transcending skills; the mechanisms that operate on the outputs of lower level modules (at whatever level such identifiable processing mechanisms emerge) must be very task specific. This involves looking at such "mechanisms" from an information-processing, rule-based perspective, of course—because it is only at the point that the system switches over from a uninterpretable, subsymbolic, non-rule-following connectionist level to an interpretable, symbolic, rule-based information-processing level that such mechanisms could be identified.

The research results reported in chapters 4 and 5 can be explained equally well by and incorporated equally easily into either a strong connectionist approach or a weak connectionist scenario that incorporates information processing at some later, higher level stage. If the strong connectionist account is the correct one, then the search for identifiable cognitive mechanisms will be a fruitless one, because there simply are no rules in the system, however much it may appear otherwise. On the other hand, if an information-processing approach remains viable—regardless of the level at which the necessary symbols and procedures emerge from what are, in all likelihood, lower level connectionist modules—then the task before us will be to identify the task-specific skills and mechanisms that lead to creative performance.

Must we know, as creativity theorists and researchers, which is the true story in order to know how to proceed? Yes and no. Yes, we need to know what the overall architecture of cognition is if we want to construct a connectionist simulation that we can plausibly believe is functioning in a way that parallels human cognition (because this is possible only under a strong connectionist answer to the question of the overall architecture of cognition). And yes, we need to know the answer to this question if we want to identify the actual information-processing mechanisms that humans employ when they perform creatively (because if information processing is wrong at all levels, as eliminative connectionism argues, then there are simply no such skills to identify).

But on the other hand, no, we do not need to know the answer to the overall architecture-of-cognition question in order to proceed with work that will help us understand creativity. Even if an information-processing approach to explaining how the brain actually operates is a myth, and even if the "skills" we identify by means of carefully controlled studies in which specific skills are taught and their effects on creative performance are measured turn out to be illusory, much can be gained by identifying such skills.

First of all, there are important practical gains. Even if we do not properly understand how such training works, if we do know what kinds of training lead reliably to higher levels of creative performance in a given task domain, then we have a potentially powerful tool for improving creativity in that domain. Even if this is all we gained from such studies, they would be well worth conducting.

However, there are also important theoretical gains that will emerge from such research, no matter which architecture-of-cognition paradigm tells the truer story. Careful identification of such cognitive skills will, at the very least, help us chart the geography of the many domains of creativity, even though, like all maps, such descriptions will tell only part of the truth, and will even incorporate some untruths. To push the map-making metaphor a bit, it is true that for many uses we prefer the convenience of flat maps to globes, even though no one believes that the world is flat (and even when we use globes, we often find it convenient to tell "lies" by way of the various lines we add that are part of the globe, but not part of the world it maps). Similarly, "mapping" the skills important to creative performance—even if such skills have only a phenomenological reality, but not a processing-level, computational reality—will help us to better understand creativity.

If the eliminative connectionist story is correct, then it may turn out that the "skills" we identify are only true from the outside of the brain looking in; what is happening on the inside would be something entirely different. It is possible that our thinking could appear as if we used certain skills—as if we followed certain rules, be they algorithmic or heuristic—even though it may turn out that we do not. In a very different field of research, Marcel (1979, 1980) suggested that phonemic analysis may have no processing reality—that we may not actually use phonemic analysis at all in understanding speech—even though phonemes are a potentially productive and workable unit for the analysis of speech that evolution might have used, had it not developed a different approach to comprehending the flow of acoustic features that make up speech. The cognitive skills that might appear, as the result of careful research, to underlie creative performance in a given task domain could, in a similar way, be illusory and yet nonetheless prove to be useful descriptions of a subsymbolic, hidden, and densely connectionist process.

Of course, the skills we identify may also turn out to be exactly the skills that humans do indeed use when thinking creatively in a given task domain—and in such a happy event, mapping these skills would provide more than the answers to the questions posed by a geographic metaphor for understanding creativity. Correctly identifying such skills would answer computational-level questions as well as questions of description. Identifying these skills would not provide the whole picture of the factors and processes leading to creative performance in a given task domain, but they would certainly provide an uncommonly rich set of answers to a wide range of questions.

There is yet another possibility for the way in which the skills we identify might match, or not match, actual human cognitive operations: The skills that we identify might be accurate descriptions of creative thinking, and thus answer well the questions asked under the geography metaphor, but different processing mechanisms than the ones we identify might actually be more accurate at the computational level. Indeed, I argue that divergent-thinking theories have been of this third class, useful in describing creative thinking but inaccurate in identifying the actual cognitive operations that are important in creative thinking.

In identifying the many skills that (at least appear to) contribute to creative performance in a particular task domain, divergent-thinking theory may still prove to be a very useful guide, especially in light of the results of Studies 6 and 7 regarding the effects of training in divergent thinking. Thus, theories of divergent thinking, and especially the various training procedures based on such theories, might be rich sources of hypotheses for task-specific creativity-relevant skills.

Divergent thinking, and the general skills of fluency, flexibility, originality, and so on that it has been hypothesized to include, may remain useful not only as ways to help identify more accurate task-specific creative-thinking skills, but also as ways to classify such skills. Fluency, to return to an example used earlier, is not the general-purpose thinking skill that divergent-thinking theories have claimed it to be; but it may be a convenient, even if sometimes misleading, way to group a wide variety of skills that are more psychologically "real" at the cognitive or computational level than is a general skill of fluency. If future research demonstrates the existence of a variety of fluency-related skills, such as those proposed earlier (e.g., "fluency in producing many words that begin with the same sound" and "fluency in inventing many metaphors for a given concept"), it may continue to be convenient at times to group them under the superordinate heading of "fluency-related skills" (or some such term that acknowledged both their similarities and their differences). Although the skills that would be grouped into this family of fluency-related skills would be cognitively different—in most cases they would, in fact, have no relationship whatsoever at the cognitive or computational level—they nonetheless have a conceptual similarity that might lead (and, in fact, has already lead) to their being considered together, as a group.

There are dangers, of course, in basing a system of classification only on its convenience or on merely superficial conceptual similarities that might, in fact, be illusory when looked at from a cognitive/computational perspective. The testing of creativity as a general skill (by testing general divergent-thinking skill) is one such danger. The results of Studies 1–7 argue strongly against the validity of any such testing (as does much previous experience with creativity testing, as outlined in chapter 3). The testing of general creative-thinking skills—whether this be done by testing general divergent-thinking skill or be measuring some other general skills or attributes—simply violates what we now know about creativity. Similarly, referring to individuals as "creative," whether as a result of divergent-thinking testing or some other, perhaps informal, assessment procedure, begs the question, "Creative doing what?" An individual may be creative in a wide variety of activities—random variation would argue that this would occur, even among a set of totally unrelated performance or task domains—but this should not be taken to mean that such a multitalented individual has some skill that leads to creative performance at many tasks. At a cognitive or computational level, creativity and creative thinking must be task-specific concepts, and the fact that we have higher level theories of creativity should not lead us to ignore this task specificity.

As long as we are aware of the purposes and limitations of higher level, noncomputational, descriptive theories of creativity, however, such theories can be quite useful. The apparently mistaken idea that divergent-thinking skills are general-purpose creative-thinking skills has already led to some productive outcomes (especially in terms of creativity-training programs). Higher level categories such as fluency (or, at a still higher level, the overarching category of divergent thinking) may make it easier to discuss a broad range of creativity-relevant phenomena and may provide a range of hypotheses for cognitive- or computational-level skills or processes. If the role of divergent-thinking theory is limited to assisting in hypothesis generation and to providing a convenient general label for groups of cognitively unrelated skills, it can make valuable contributions to creativity research and theory. As long as their limitations at the cognitive level are borne in mind, general theories of creativity—including, and perhaps especially, the divergent-thinking theories—should continue to play a productive role in increasing our understanding of the nature of creativity.

# Appendix A: Instructions Given to Judges

Poetry- and story-writing tests:

There is only one criterion in rating these tests: creativity. I realize that creativity doesn't exist in a vacuum, and to some extent creativity probably overlaps other criteria one might apply—aesthetic appeal, organization, richness of imagery, sophistication of expression, novelty of word choice, appropriateness of word choice, and possibly even correctness of grammar, for example—but I ask you to rank the poems (stories) solely on the basis of your thoughtful-but-subjective opinions of their creativity. The point is, you are the expert, and you needn't defend your choices or articulate a definition of creativity. What creativity means to you can remain a mystery—what I want you to do is use that mysterious expert sense to rank order the poems (stories) for creativity.

Equation- and word-problem-creating tests:

There is only one criterion in rating these tests: creativity. I realize that creativity doesn't exist in a vacuum, and to some extent creativity probably overlaps other criteria one might apply—degree of difficulty, novelty, aesthetic appeal, usefulness in teaching a concept, appropriateness, and precision, for example—but I ask you to rank the equations (word problems) solely on the basis of your thoughtful-but-subjective opinions of their creativity. The point is, you are the expert, and you needn't defend your choices or articulate a definition of creativity. What creativity means to you can remain a mystery—what I want you to do is use that mysterious expert sense to rank order the equations (word problems) for creativity.

Collage-making test:

There is only one criterion in rating these collages: creativity. I realize that creativity doesn't exist in a vacuum, and to some extent creativity probably overlaps other criteria one might apply—aesthetic appeal, organization, use of color, novelty, complexity, balance, symmetry, technical goodness, neatness, or detail, for example—but I ask you to rate the collages solely on the basis of your thoughtful-but-subjective opinions of their creativity. The point is, you are the expert, and you needn't defend your choices or articulate a definition of creativity. What creativity means to you can remain a mystery—what I want you to do is use that mysterious expert sense to rate the collages for creativity.

Storytelling test:

There is only one criterion in rating these stories: creativity. I realize that creativity doesn't exist in a vacuum, and to some extent creativity probably overlaps other criteria one might apply—aesthetic appeal, organization, richness of imagery, sophistication of expression, novelty of word choice, appropriateness of word choice, and possibly even correctness of grammar, for example—but I ask you to rate the stories solely on the basis of your thoughtful-but-subjective opinions of their creativity. The point is, you are the expert, and you needn't defend your choices or articulate a definition of creativity. What creativity means to you can remain a mystery—what I want you to do is use that mysterious expert sense to rate the stories for creativity.

# Appendix B: Description of the Judges

The judges for Studies 1 and 5 included several college mathematics and English professors, poets, a mathematics graduate student, secondary mathematics and language arts teachers, a school-system supervisor of language arts, a school-system supervisor of mathematics, and a school-system writing specialist. The judges for Studies 2, 3, 4, 6, and 7 were elementary-school teachers, specialists in gifted education, and art educators (for the collages). In all cases, the judges were experts in the domains in which they served as judges, and in no case did they know the students whose papers they were rating. All judges worked independently and were paid for their work.

In Study 7, three of the five judges for the story-writing, story-telling, poetry-writing, and word-problem tests rated all four tests. The other 22 judges each rated one test each. (Two rated only the poems, two rated only the written stories, two rated only the tape-recorded stories, and 14 rated the collages.) This overlap may have contributed to the correlations among the verbal tests (as shown in Tables 5.8 and 5.11). There is no way to calculate the size of this possible effect, or even to determine if there was any such effect; however, to the extent that this judge overlap influenced test scores, it would in all likelihood have increased, rather than decreased, their size, and would not, therefore, weaken (but would in fact strengthen) the conclusion that the observed pattern of correlations does not provide evidence of any general creativity-relevant factor.

# Appendix C: Sample Stories, Poems, and Word Problems Created by Subjects in Study 7

Following are samples of the stories subjects told and the stories, poems, and word problems they wrote. In each case, at least one sample that received a fairly low creativity score and one that received a fairly high creativity score are included. The mean score of the judges (on a 1.00–5.00 scale) and the group of the subject who created each of the samples are noted.

## STORYTELLING TEST

Subject number 02; control group; mean rating = 1.5

A boy went fishing. He caught something. He reeled it in. He fell into the water. He is in the pond. A turtle has the hook. The dog comes out and barks at the turtle. The boy comes out. The turtle snaps the dog's paw. The boy picks up the dog. He walks in the pond. He is walking farther in the pond. He is on the land. He is bending down to put down his bucket, shovel, and fishing rod. The turtle bites the dog's tail. The turtle pulls the dog in. The dog is in the pond. The only thing left is the dog's leg. The boy goes in after him. He got the dog out. The dog looks at the turtle. The boy grabs the turtle with .... The turtle grabs the boy's rod. The boy gets the turtle. The boy goes home. The boy digs. The boy finds something. He didn't dig hard. The boy puts a flower in there. The turtle holds the rod. The boy holds up the turtle, and the frog jumps. They walk home.

Subject number 01; control group; mean rating = 2.8

A little boy went fishing one day, and he caught something. He tried to pull it out of the water. It pulled him in the water. He found out it was a turtle, and it pulled his fishing rod away. His dog barked at the turtle. The turtle bit the dog hard. The little boy tried to pull the dog away from the turtle. The turtle stayed on the dog, and the turtle fell into the water. He let go of the dog. The dog licked his paw. The turtle bit the dog's tail. The turtle pulled the dog in the water. The dog was falling into the water, and the boy was getting ready to go swimming to save the dog, he got right ready to save the dog and the dog came up out of the water, and the turtle was playing dead in the water, and he saved the turtle, and he carried the turtle and he was digging a hole for the turtle. And the turtle was laying on the back of his shell, and he turned over and he got the stick. He started holding the stick, and he was still alive, and the dog and everyone was happy, and then they went home.

Subject number 28; control group; mean rating = 3.0

Once upon a time there was a boy. He was fishing at a pond, and he thought he caught something. And he felt a big tug, and the tug pulled him into the water. Then he got angry, and then he saw a turtle. The dog and the turtle were fighting. Then the little boy saw what was going on. He was surprised. Then he picked up the dog and the turtle and he walked away. And then he took the fishing pole and the dog and the turtle and went down the pond, then he went on shore, and then he started to dig. Then he saw the frog and the dog. The dog fell into the water. The frog went into the water, too. The boy was going to go in, too. The boy changed his mind, and then he thought for a minute, then he tickled the turtle and the frog was sitting there on the lily pad. The boy was going home. Then he started to dig again. He planted a flower there, and then he admired the flower. And he picked up the turtle and the dog.

Subject number 21; experimental group; mean rating = 4.6

Once there was a boy named Robert and a dog named Spot and a frog named Wilford, and they went out fishing. The boy thought he'd caught something, but he couldn't pull it out. He fell in, and so did the dog and the frog.

When they saw what was pulling on the fish rod, it was a big, fat turtle. The dog swam up and yelled at it, but all the turtle did was bite its paw. The turtle wouldn't let go. The boy had to carry him back to where they were fishing, and then the turtle fell off.

They started fishing again. The dog licked his paw, and then he felt something, and the big, fat turtle was pulling on its tail. The boy said, "Oh, no!" The dog fell in again. All you could see was his left foot sticking out, and then you couldn't see him at all. Then the only thing that came up was his face, and then he got out.

They saw the turtle floating in the water on its back. They thought he was dead, but he was only tricking. They got him and dug him a grave. They were about to put him in when he got the fishing rod and was walking away, and then he walked toward them. Then he wanted to be their friend, so the boy lifted him up, and everybody shouted, "HOORAY!"

The turtle took the fishing rod and brought it home—he held it all the way home—and the frog sat on its back.

And that's the end.

## STORY-WRITING TEST

Subject number 38; control group; mean rating = 1.5

### The Story About Jack and Jill

There was a boy and girl. They both liked to dance. They boy was named Jack and the girl was named Jill and they had cookies and milk and they got dressed up and they had so much fun.

Subject number 05; experimental group; mean rating = 1.9

One day a boy and a girl named Jack and Jill went on a picnic. When they had finished, they started to dance. First they took off their shoes, and then they danced. When they finished dancing they fell asleep.

Subject number 10; experimental group; mean rating = 3.4

Once there was a boy and a girl. They had lots of fun, they would just do everything together. They would go on picnics in the parks, they would dress up and dance, and that's only some of the things they did together. One day they had a picnic and they brought clothes to dance in. They ate their lunch and then they got dressed up and started dancing. People stared at them but they didn't care, but it was pretty weird. Then they were so tired out that they had to sit down and they had milk and cookies and then they walked home. And they were so tired out that when they got home they took a nap. And since they had so much fun that day they were planning to do the same exact thing the next day.

Subject number 06; experimental group; mean rating = 4.0

One day Jake and Jill were having a picnic and they began to dance. They took their shoes off, too. They knocked over their food and their tea and their cakes and milk. Jake and Jill did not stop dancing for a long time. Then one day a man came over to them and said, "What are you doing?" Jake said, "Dancing." "Oh," said the man. One day they stopped dancing and Jill said, "I'm hungry." "Me, too," said Jake.

One day they played the lottery and they won one thousand dollars and they started to dance again. Then one day they moved into a big castle.

And they lived happily ever after.

Subject number 15 (whose work on the Word-Problem Creating Test is also sampled later); experimental group; mean rating = 4.0

Once upon a time, deep in the woods, there lived two kids named Bebop and

RockSteady.

They were brother and sister and they liked each other a lot.

One day they were bored. So RockSteady said, "Let's dance." Then Bebop replied, "We don't have music." "So let's find some," said RockSteady. Before you could say "Gee Whittakers" they were gone looking for music. They searched and searched and searched, then finally RockSteady spotted something gray. "Look, a radio!" shouted RockSteady. "Oh, great!" said Bebop. "Now we can dance!" So they turned on the radio and danced till they dropped.


## POETRY-WRITING TEST

Subject number 35; control group; mean rating = 1.3

Roses are red
Violets are blue
Who do I love
I love you


Subject number 03; experimental group; mean rating = 3.1

### Trees

In the winter trees frost their branches. In the spring trees grow their leaves back. In the fall leaves fall and their leaves turn all different colors. In the summer tree leaves are dark green. Trees are something nice and that is why God made the tree.

Subject number 25; control group; mean rating = 3.2

### 1 2 3's

One, two, three, is as easy as can be, four, five six, is harder than sticks, seven, eight, nine, nine is the queen, and eight is the prince, but ten is the king.

Subject number 19; experimental group; mean rating = 4.6

### The Mouse

There once was a mouse
that ate a house
made out of cheese
and oh did he sneeze

he thought it might be allergies
but he was not quite sure
so he ate a frookie cookie
and that was his cure.

## WORD-PROBLEM CREATING TEST

Subject number 15 (whose work on the Story-Writing Test is also sampled earlier); experimental group; mean rating = 2.5

Mike went to the store.
He had 25 cents.
There was a stamp for 5 cents.
He bought it.
How much did he have left?

Subject number 23; control group; mean rating = 2.9

Once there were 20 flying dogs. 10 landed. How many left?
12 more flew in. How many flying now?

Subject number 10; experimental group; mean rating = 3.9

Theresa was buying some hay for her horse. She got to the place. There were two different kinds and one cost $10.00, the other cost $6.15. She only had $7.00. She bought the one for $6.15. How much did she have left?

Subject number 26; control group; mean rating = 5.0

How much rope would it take to wrap around the Twin Towers? They are both the same size and height. They are each 1,000½ feet around. The height is the same on each of them. Each is 100,000 feet tall.

# REFERENCES

Amabile, T. M. (1979). Effects of external evaluation on creativity. *Journal of Personality and Social Psychology, 37,* 221–233.

Amabile, T. M. (1982). Social psychology of creativity: A consensual assessment technique. *Journal of Personality and Social Psychology, 43,* 997–1013.

Amabile, T. M. (1983). *The social psychology of creativity.* New York: Springer-Verlag.

Amabile, T. M., Hennessey, B. A., Grossman, B. S. (1986). Social influences on creativity: The effects of contracted-for reward. *Journal of Personality and Social Psychology, 50,* 14–23.

Anastasi, A. (1982). *Psychological testing.* New York: Macmillan.

Anderson, J. R. (1980). *Cognitive psychology and its implications.* San Francisco: W. H. Freeman.

Baer, J. (1988a). Artificial intelligence: Making machines that think. *Futurist, 22*(1), 8–13.

Baer, J. (1988b). Long-term effects of creativity training with middle school students. *Journal of Early Adolescence, 8,* 183–193.

Baer, J. (1991). Generality of creativity across performance domains. *Creativity Research Journal, 4,* 23–39.

Baer, J. (1992, August). *Divergent thinking is not a general trait: A multi-domain training experiment.* Paper presented at the annual meeting of the American Psychological Association, Washington, DC.

Bamberger, J. (1990). Current views on research in creativity. *Contemporary Psychology, 35,* 434–435.

Belenky, M. F., Clinchy, B. M., Goldberger, N. R., & Tarule, J. M. (1986). *Women's ways of knowing: The development of self, voice, and mind.* New York: Basic Books.

Bereiter, C. (1991). Implications of connectionism for thinking about rules. *Educational Researcher, 20*(3), 10–16.

Bella Vista Elementary School. (1965). *Project Implode.* Salt Lake City, UT: Author.

Binet, A. (1962). The nature and measurement of intelligence. In L. Postman (Ed.), *Psychology in the making: Histories of selected research programs.* New York: Knopf. (Original work published 1911)

Bjorklund, D. (1985). The role of conceptual knowledge in the development of organization in children's memory. In C. J. Brainerd & M. Pressley (Eds.), *Basic processes in memory development research* (pp. 103–142). New York: Springer-Verlag.

Boorstin, D. J. (1958). *The Americans: The colonial experience.* New York: Random House.

Boring. E. G. (1923). Intelligence as the tests test it. *New Republic, 34,* 35–37.

Borland, J. H. (1986). A note on the existence of certain divergent- production abilities. *Journal for the Education of the Gifted, 9,* 239–251.

Brandt, R. (1992). On research and teaching: A conversation with Lee Schulman. *Educational Leadership, 49*(7), 14–19.

Brown, A. L., Bransford, J. D., Ferrara, R. A., & Campione, J. C. (1983). Learning, remembering, and understanding. In P. H. Mussen (series Ed.) & J. H. Flavell & E. M. Markman (Vol. Eds.), *Handbook of cognitive development* (Vol. 3, pp. 77–166). New York: Wiley.

Brown, A. L., Campione, J. C., & Barclay, C. R. (1979). Training self- checking routines for estimating test readiness: Generalization from list learning to prose recall. *Child Development, 50,* 501–512.

Cantor, N., & Kihlstrom, J. (1987). *Personality and social intelligence.* Englewood Cliffs, NJ: Prentice-Hall.

Cattell, R. B., & Cattell, A. K. (1963). *Test of g: Culture fair, Scale 3.* Champaign, IL: Institute for Personality and Ability Testing.

Chi, M. T. H. (1978). Knowledge structures and memory development. In R. Siegler (Ed.), *Children's thinking: What develops?* Hillsdale, NJ: Lawrence Erlbaum Associates.

Christensen, P. R., Guilford, J. P., Merrifield, P. R., & Wilson, R. C. (1978). *Alternate uses.* Orange, CA: Sheridan Psychological Services.

Churchland, P. M. (1988). *Matter and consciousness.* Cambridge, MA: MIT Press.

Churchland, P. S. (1989). From Descartes to neural networks. *Scientific American, 261*(1), 118.

Cohen, J., & Cohen, P. (1983). *Applied multiple regression/correlation analysis for the behavioral sciences* (2nd ed.). Hillsdale, NJ: Lawrence Erlbaum Associates.

Connecticut State Department of Education. (1988). *Connecticut Assessment of Educational Progress.* (Available from Joan Baron, Connecticut State Department of Education/Office of Research and Evaluation, P.O. Box 2219, Hartford, CT 06145)

Costa, A. L. (Ed.). (1985). *Developing minds: A resource book for teaching thinking.* Alexandria, VA: Association for Supervision and Curriculum Development.

Covington, M. V., Crutchfield, R. S., Davies, L. B., & Olton, R. M. (1974). *The productive thinking program.* Columbus, OH: Merrill.

Crabbe, A. B. (1985). Future problem solving. In A. L. Costa (Ed.), *Developing minds: A resource book for teaching thinking* (pp. 217–219). Alexandria, VA: Association for Supervision and Curriculum Development.

Crockenberg, S. B. (1972). Creativity tests: A boon or boondoggle for education? *Review of Educational Research, 42,* 27–45.

Cropley, A. J. (1972). A five-year longitudinal study of the validity of creativity tests. *Developmental Psychology, 6,* 119–124.

Csikszentmihalyi, M. (1988). Society, culture, and person: A systems view of creativity. In R. J. Sternberg (Ed.), *The nature of creativity* (pp. 325–339). Cambridge University Press.

Csikszentmihalyi, M. (1990). The domain of creativity. In M. A. Runco & R. S. Albert (Eds.), *Theories of creativity* (pp. 190–212). Newbury Park, CA: Sage.

Darley, J. M., Glucksberg, S., & Kinchla, R. A. (1986). *Psychology* (3rd ed.). Englewood Cliffs, NJ: Prentice-Hall.

Davies, P. (1984). *Superforce: The search for a grand unified theory of nature.* New York: Simon & Schuster.

de Bono, E. (1985). The CoRT Thinking Program. In A. L. Costa (Ed.), *Developing minds: A resource book for teaching thinking* (pp. 203–209). Alexandria, VA: Association for Supervision and Curriculum Development.

DeLisi, R., & Staudt, J. (1980). Individual differences in college students' performance on formal operational tasks. *Journal of Applied Developmental Psychology, 1,* 201–208.

Dennett, D. C. (1986). *Brainstorms: Philosophical essays on mind and psychology.* Cambridge, MA: MIT Press.

Dennett, D. C. (1991). *Consciousness explained.* Boston: Little, Brown.

Draper, W. D. (1985). A cursory review of current creativity research. *Creative Child & Adult Quarterly, 10,* 86–89.

Eberle, B., & Stanish, B. (1980). *CPS for kids: A resource book for teaching creative problem-solving to children.* Buffalo, NY: D.O.K. Publishers.

Edelman, G. M. (1987). *Neural Darwinism: The theory of neuronal group selection.* New York: Basic Books.

Edelman, G. M. (1989). *The remembered present: A biological theory of consciousness.* New York: Basic Books.

Fausto-Sterling, A. (1991). Race, gender, and science. *Transformations, 2*(2), 4–12.

Feldhusen, J. F., Treffinger, D. J., & Bahlke, S. J. (1970). Developing creative thinking: The Purdue creativity program. *Journal of creative behavior, 4,* 85–90.

Fivush, R., & Hudson, J. A. (1990). *Knowing and remembering in young children.* Cambridge: Cambridge University Press.

Flavell, J. H. (1970). Developmental studies of mediated memory. In H. W. Reese & L. P. Lipsitt (Eds.),

*Advances in child development and behavior* (Vol. 5, pp. 182–211). New York: Academic Press.

Flavell, J. H. (1985). *Cognitive development* (2nd ed.). Englewood Cliffs, NJ: Prentice-Hall.

Flavell, J. H., & Wellman, H. M. (1977). Metamemory. In R. V. Kail & J. W. Hagen (Eds.), *Perspectives on the development of memory and cognition* (pp. 3–33). Hillsdale, NJ: Lawrence Erlbaum Associates.

Gardner, H. (1983). *Frames of mind: The theory of multiple intelligences.* New York: Basic Books.

Gardner, H. (1985). *The mind's new science: A history of the cognitive revolution.* New York: Basic Books.

Gardner, H. (1988). Creative lives and creative works: A synthetic scientific approach. In R. J. Sternberg (Ed.), *The nature of creativity* (pp. 298–321). Cambridge University Press.

Gardner, H. (1989). *To open minds.* New York: Basic Books.

Garner, R., & Reis, R. (1981). Monitoring and resolving comprehension obstacles: An investigation of spontaneous text lookbacks among upper-grade good and poor comprehenders. *Reading Research Quarterly, 16,* 569–582.

Gilligan, C. (1982). *In a different voice: Psychological theory and women's development.* Harvard University Press.

Gilligan, C., & Attanucci, J. (1988). Two moral orientations. In C. Gilligan, J. V. Ward, & J. M. Taylor (Eds.), *Mapping the moral domain* (pp. 73–86). Cambridge, MA: Harvard University Press.

Glass, A. L., & Holyoak, K. J. (1986). *Cognition* (2nd ed.). New York: Random House.

Gordon, W. J. J. (1961). *Synectics.* New York: Harper & Row.

Gourley, T. J. (1981). Adapting the varsity sports model to nonpsychomotor gifted students. *Gifted Child Quarterly, 25*(4), 164–166.

Gruber, H. E. (1981) *Darwin on man: A psychological study of scientific creativity* (2nd ed.). University of Chicago Press.

Gruber, H. E., & Davis, S. N. (1988). Inching our way up Mount Olympus: The evolving-systems approach to creative thinking. In R. J. Sternberg (Ed.), *The nature of creativity* (pp. 243–270). Cambridge University Press.

Guilford, J. P. (1950). Creativity. *American Psychologist, 14,* 205–208.

Guilford, J. P. (1956). The structure of intellect. *Psychological Bulletin, 53,* 267–293.

Guilford, J. P. (1967). *The nature of human intelligence.* New York: McGraw-Hill.

Guilford, J. P., & Hoepfner, R. (1971). *The analysis of intelligence.* New York: McGraw-Hill.

Hagen, J. W., & Stanovich, K. E. (1977). Memory: Strategies of acquisition. In R. V. Kail & J. W. Hagen (Eds.), *Perspectives on the development of memory and cognition* (pp. 89–112). Hillsdale, NJ: Lawrence Erlbaum Associates.

Harding, S. (1986). *The science question in feminism.* Ithaca, NY: Cornell University Press.

Hattie, J. (1980). Should creativity tests be administered under testlike conditions? An empirical study of three alternative conditions. *Journal of Educational Psychology, 72,* 87–98.

Hawking, S. W. (1988). *A brief history of time: From the big bang to black holes.* New York: Bantam.

Heausler, N. L., & Thompson, B. (1988). Structure of the Torrance Tests of Creative Thinking. *Educational and Psychological Measurement, 48,* 463–468.

Hennessey, B. A., & Amabile, T. M. (1988a). Conditions of creativity. In R. J. Sternberg (Ed.), *The nature of creativity* (pp. 11–38). Cambridge: Cambridge University Press.

Hennessey, B. A., & Amabile, T. M. (1988b). Story-telling: A method for assessing children's creativity. *Journal of Creative Behavior, 22,* 235–246.

Hocevar, D. (1976). Dimensions of creativity. *Psychological Reports, 39,* 869–870.

Hocevar, D. (1978). Studies in the evaluation of tests of divergent thinking (Doctoral Dissertation, Cornell University, 1977). *Dissertation Abstracts International, 38,* 4685A–4686A.

Hocevar, D. (1979). The unidimensional nature of creative thinking in fifth-grade children. *Child Study Journal, 9,* 273–278.

Hocevar, D. (1980). Intelligence, divergent thinking, and creativity. *Intelligence, 4,* 25–40.

Hofstadter, D. R. (1985). *Metamagical themes: Questing for the essence of mind and pattern.* New York: Basic Books.

Hoomes, E. W. (1986). Future problem solving: Preparing students for a world community. *Gifted Education International, 4*(1), 16– 20.

Isaksen, S. G., & Parnes, S. J. (1985). Curriculum planning for creative behavior and problem solving. *Journal of Creative Behavior, 19,* 1–28.

Jeffrey, L. (1983). *The thinker as poet: A psychological study of the creative process through an analysis of a poet's worksheets.* Unpublished doctoral dissertation, Rutgers University, Newark, NJ.

Jensen, A. R. (1980). *Bias in mental testing.* New York: Free Press.

Johnson-Laird, P. N. (1987). Reasoning, imagining, and creating. *Bulletin of the British Psychological Society, 40,* 121–129.

Johnson-Laird, P. N. (1988a). *The computer and the mind.* Cambridge, MA: Harvard University Press.

Johnson-Laird, P. N. (1988b). Freedom and constraint in creativity. In R. J. Sternberg (Ed.), *The nature of creativity* (pp. 202–219). Cambridge: Cambridge University Press.

Jordan, L. (1975). Use of canonical analysis in Cropley's "A five-year longitudinal study of the validity of creativity tests." *Developmental Psychology, 11,* 1–3.

Kagan, D. M. (1988). Measurements of divergent and complex thinking. *Educational and Psychological Measurement, 48,* 873– 884.

Kail, R. V., Jr., & Siegel, A. W. (1977). The development of mnemonic encoding in children: From perception to abstraction. In R. V. Kail & J. W. Hagen (Eds.), *Perspectives on the development of memory and cognition* (pp. 61–88). Hillsdale, NJ: Lawrence Erlbaum Associates.

Kaplan, P. S. (1990). *Educational psychology for tomorrow's teacher.* St. Paul, MN: West Publishing.

Kogan, N. (1983). Stylistic variation in childhood and adolescence: Creativity, metaphor, and cognitive styles. In P. H. Mussen (Ed.), *Handbook of child psychology: Vol 3. Cognitive development* (4th ed., pp. 628–706). New York: Wiley.

Kogan, N, & Pankove, E. (1974). Long-term predictive validity of divergent-thinking tests. *Journal of Educational Psychology, 66,* 802–810.

Kramer, D. A., & Bopp, M. J. (Eds.). (1989). Transformation in clinical and developmental psychology. New York: Springer-Verlag.

Kuhn, T. S. (1970). *The structure of scientific revolutions.* University of Chicago Press.

Lange, G. (1978). Organizational processes in children's recall. In P. A. Ornstein (Ed.), *Memory development in children* (pp. 101–128). Hillsdale, NJ: Lawrence Erlbaum Associates.

Langley, P., & Jones, R. (1988). Computational models of scientific thought. In R. J. Sternberg (Ed.), *The nature of creativity* (pp. 177–201). Cambridge: Cambridge University Press.

Langley, P., Simon, H. A., Bradshaw, G. L., & Zytkow, J. M. (1987). *Scientific discovery: Computational explorations of the creative process.* Cambridge, MA: MIT Press.

Lissitz, R. W., & Willhoft, J. L. (1985). A methodological study of the Torrance Tests of Creativity. *Journal of Educational Measurement, 22,* 1–11.

Maltzman, I. (1960). On the training of originality. *Psychological Review, 67,* 229–242.

Maltzman, I., Belloni, M., & Fishbein, M. (1964). Experimental studies of associative variables in originality. *Psychological Monographs, 78*(3, Whole No. 580).

Maltzman, I., Bogartz, W., & Breger, L. (1958). A procedure for increasing association originality and its transfer effects. *Journal of Experimental Psychology, 56,* 393–398.

Maltzman, I., Brooks, L. O., Bogartz, W., & Summers, S. S. (1958). The facilitation of problem solving by prior exposure to uncommon responses. *Journal of Experimental Psychology, 56,* 399–406.

Maltzman, I., Simon, S. Raskin, D., & Licht, L. (1960). Experimental studies in the training of originality. *Psychological Monographs, 74*(6, Whole No. 493).

Mansfield, R. S., Busse, T. V., & Krepelka, E. J. (1978). The effectiveness of creativity training. *Review of Educational Research, 48,* 517–536.

Marcel, A. J. (1979). Phonological awareness and phonological representation: Investigation of a specific spelling problem. In U. Frith (Ed.), *Cognitive processes in spelling* (pp. 373–403). New York: Academic Press.

Marcel, A. J. (1980). Conscious and unconscious perception: An approach to the relations between phenomenal experience and perceptual processes. *Cognitive Psychology, 15,* 238–300.

Markman, E. M. (1985). Comprehension monitoring: Developmental and educational issues. In S. F. Chipman, J. W. Segal, & R. Glaser (Eds.), *Thinking and learning skills: Volume 2, Research and open questions* (pp. 275–291). Hillsdale, NJ: Lawrence Erlbaum Associates.

Mayer, M. (1967). *A boy, a dog, and a frog.* New York: Dial Press.

Mayer, M., & Mayer, M. (1971). *A boy, a dog, a frog, and a friend.* New York: Dial Press.

Mayer, R. E. (1983). *Thinking, problem solving, cognition.* New York: W. H. Freeman.

Mayer, R. E. (1987). *Educational psychology: A cognitive approach.* Boston: Little, Brown.

McClelland, J. L., Rumelhart, D. E., & the PDP Research Group (Eds.). (1986). *Parallel distributed processing: Explorations in the microstructure of cognition. Vol. 2. Psychological and biological models.* Cambridge, MA: MIT Press.

McCrae, R.R., Arenberg, D., & Costa, P.T., Jr. (1987). Declines in divergent thinking with age: Cross-sectional, longitudinal, and cross-sequential analyses. *Psychology and Aging, 2*(2), 1–8.

McKerrow, K. K., & McKerrow, J. E. (1991). Naturalistic misunderstanding of the Heisenberg Uncertainty Principle. *Educational Researcher, 20*(1), 17–20.

McShane, J. (1991). *Cognitive development: An information- processing approach.* Cambridge, MA: Basil Blackwell.

Mednick, S. A. (1962). The associative basis of the creative process. *Psychological Review, 69,* 220–232.

Mednick, S. A., and Mednick, M. T. (1967). *Examiner's manual: Remote Associates Test.* Boston: Houghton Mifflin.

Meeker, M. (1969). *The SOI: Its uses and interpretations.* Columbus, OH: Merrill.

Meeker, M. (1985). SOI. In A. L. Costa (Ed.), *Developing minds: A resource book for teaching thinking* (pp. 187–192). Alexandria, VA: Association for Supervision and Curriculum Development.

Micklus, C. S. (1986). *OM-AHA!: Problems to develop creative thinking skills.* Glassboro, NJ: Creative Competitions.

Micklus, C. S., & Micklus, C. (1986). *OM program handbook.* Glassboro, NJ: Creative Competitions.

Miikkulainen, R., & Dyer, M. G. (1991). Natural language processing with modular PDP networks and distributed lexicon. *Cognitive Science, 15,* 343–399.

Minsky, M. (1986). *The society of mind.* New York: Simon & Schuster.

Mobile County Public Schools. (1974). *TAP: A Talents Unlimited demonstration project.* Mobile, AL: Author.

Myers, R. E., & Torrance, E. P. (1964). *Invitations to thinking and doing.* Lexington, MA: Ginn.

National Talent Network. (1989). *Gifted programs from the National Talent Network.* Sewell, NJ: Author.

Nelson, L. H. (1990). *Who knows: From Quine to a feminist empiricism.* Philadelphia: Temple University Press.

Norman, D. A.. (1986). Reflections on cognition and parallel distributed processing. In J. L. McClelland, D. E. Rumelhart, & the PDP Research Group (Eds.), *Parallel distributed processing: Explorations in the microstructure of cognition. Vol. 2. Psychological and biological models* (pp. 531–552). Cambridge, MA: MIT Press.

Nunnally, J. C. (1978). *Psychometric theory* (2nd ed.). New York: McGraw-Hill.

Olton, R. M., & Crutchfield, R. S. (1969). Developing skills of productive thinking. In P. Mussen, J. Langer, & M. Covington (Eds.), *Trends and issues in developmental psychology* (pp. 68–91). New York: Holt, Rinehart & Winston.

Oon-Chye, Y., & Bridgham, R. G. (1971, April). *The interpretation of Torrance creativity scores.* Paper presented at the annual meeting of California Educational Research Association, San Diego. (ERIC Document Reproduction Service No. ED 052 254).

Ornstein, P. A., Baker-Ward, L., & Naus, M. J. (1988). The development of mnemonic skill. In F. E. Weinert & M. Perlmutter (Eds.), *Memory development: Universal changes and individual differences* (pp. 31–50). Hillsdale, NJ: Lawrence Erlbaum Associates.

Ornstein, P. A., & Naus, M. J. (1978). Rehearsal process in children's memory. In P. A. Ornstein (Ed.), *Memory development in children* (pp. 69–99). Hillsdale, NJ: Lawrence Erlbaum Associates.

Ornstein, P. A., Naus, M. J., & Stone, B. P. (1977). Rehearsal training and developmental differences in memory. *Developmental Psychology, 13,* 15–24.

Osborn, A. F. (1963). *Applied imagination.* New York: Scribner's.

Parnes, S. J. (1972). *Creativity: Unlocking human potential.* Buffalo, NY: D. O. K. Publishers.

Parnes, S. J. (1985). Creative problem solving. In A. L. Costa (Ed.), *Developing minds: A resource book for teaching thinking* (pp. 230–232). Alexandria, VA: Association for Supervision and Curriculum Development.

Parnes, S. J., & Noller, R. B. (1973). *Toward supersanity.* Buffalo, NY: D. O. K. Publishers.

Parnes, S. J., & Noller, R. B. (1974). *Toward supersanity: Research supplement.* Buffalo, NY: D. O. K. Publishers.

Perkins, D. N. (1981). *The mind's best work.* Cambridge, MA: Harvard University Press.

Pinker, S., & Prince, A. (1988). *On language and connectionism: Analysis of a parallel distributed processing model of language acquisition.* (Occasional Paper No. 33). Cambridge, MA: Center for Cognitive Science, MIT.

Pintrich, P. R. (1990). Implications of psychological research on student learning and college teaching for teacher education. In W. R. Houston, M. Haberman, & J. Sikula (Eds.), *Handbook of research on teacher education* (pp. 826–857). New York: Macmillan.

Riordan, M., & Schramm, D. N. (1991). *The shadows of creation: Dark matter and the structure of the universe.* New York: W. H. Freeman.

Rose, L. H., & Lin, H. (1984). A meta-analysis of long-term creativity training programs. *Journal of Creative Behavior, 18,* 11–22.

Rubenson, D. L., & Runco, M. A. (in press). The psychoeconomic approach to creativity. *New Ideas in Psychology.*

Rubinstein, M. F. (1975). *Patterns of problem-solving.* Englewood Cliffs, NJ: Prentice-Hall.

Rubinstein, M. F. (1980). A decade of experience in teaching an interdisciplinary problem-solving course. In D. T. Tuma & F. Reid (Eds.), *Problem solving and education: Issues in teaching and research* (pp. 25–38). Hillsdale, NJ: Lawrence Erlbaum Associates.

Rumelhart, D. E., & McClelland, J. L. (1986a). On learning the past tense of English verbs. In J. L. McClelland, D. E. Rumelhart, & the PDP Research Group (Eds.), *Parallel distributed processing: Explorations in the microstructure of cognition. Vol. 2. Psychological and biological models* (pp. 216–271). Cambridge, MA: MIT Press.

Rumelhart, D. E., & McClelland, J. L. (1986b). PDP models and general issues in cognitive science. In D. E. Rumelhart, J. L. McClelland, & the PDP Research Group (Eds.), *Parallel distributed processing: Explorations in the microstructure of cognition: Vol. 1. Foundations* (pp. 110–146). Cambridge, MA: MIT Press.

Rumelhart, D. E. McClelland, J. L., & the PDP Research Group (Eds.). (1986). *Parallel distributed processing: Explorations in the microstructure of cognition: Vol. 1. Foundations.* Cambridge, MA: MIT Press.

Runco, M. A. (1986a). The discriminant validity of gifted children's divergent thinking test scores. *Gifted Child Quarterly, 30,* 78–82.

Runco, M. A. (1986b). Divergent thinking and creative performance in gifted and nongifted children. *Educational and Psychological Measurement, 46,* 375–384.

Runco, M. A. (1986c). Predicting children's creative performance. *Psychological Reports, 59,* 1247–1254.

Runco, M. A. (1987). The generality of creative performance in gifted and nongifted children. *Gifted Child Quarterly, 31,* 121–125.

Runco, M. A. (1989). The creativity of children's art. *Child Study Journal, 19,* 177–190.

Runco, M. A. (1990). Implicit theories and ideational creativity. In M. A. Runco & R. S. Albert (Eds.), *Theories of creativity* (pp. 234–252). Newbury Park, CA: Sage.

Runco, M. A. (1991a). On economic theories of creativity. *Creativity Research Journal, 4,* 198–200.

Runco, M. A. (1991b). The evaluative, valuative, and divergent thinking of children. *Journal of Creative Behavior, 25,* 311–319.

Runco, M. A., & Albert, R. S. (1990). *Theories of creativity.* Newbury Park, CA: Sage.

Searle, J. (1980). Minds, brains, and programs. *Behavioral and Brain Sciences, 3,* 417–457.

Simon, H. A. (1967). Understanding creativity. In J. C. Gowan, G. D. Demos, & E. P. Torrance (Eds.), *Creativity: Its educational implications* (pp. 43–53). New York: Wiley.

Smiley, S. S., & Brown, A. L. (1979). Conceptual preference for thematic or taxonomic relations: A nonmonotonic age trend from preschool to old age. *Journal of Experimental Child Psychology, 30,* 249–257.

Smith, K. L. R., Michael, W. B., & Hocevar, D. (1990). Performance on creativity measures with examination-taking instructions intended to induce high or low levels of test anxiety. *Creativity Research Journal, 3,* 265–280.

Smith, L. B., Sera, M., & Gattuso, B. (1988). The development of thinking. In R. J. Sternberg & E. E. Smith (Eds.), *The psychology of human thought* (pp. 366–391). Cambridge: Cambridge University Press.

Smolensky, P. (1988). On the proper treatment of connectionism. *Behavioral and Brain Sciences, 11,* 1–23.

Snow, R. E., & Lohman, D. F. (1984). Toward a theory of cognitive aptitude for learning from instruction. *Journal of Educational Psychology, 76,* 347–376.

Spearman, C. (1927). *The abilities of man.* New York: Macmillan.

Sternberg, R. J. (1988). Intelligence. In R. J. Sternberg & E. E. Smith (Eds.), *The psychology of human thought* (pp. 267–308). Cambridge: Cambridge University Press.

Sternberg, R. J. (1990). *Metaphors of mind.* Cambridge: Cambridge University Press.

Sternberg, R. J., & Davidson, J. E. (1986). Conceptions of giftedness: A map of the terrain. In R. J. Sternberg & J. E. Davidson (Eds.), *Conceptions of giftedness* (pp. 3–18). Cambridge: Cambridge University Press.

Sternberg, R. J., & Lubart, T. I. (1991). An investment theory of creativity and its development. *Human Development, 34,* 1–31.

Tardif, T. Z., & Sternberg, R. J. (1988). What do we know about creativity? In R. J. Sternberg (Ed.), *The nature of creativity* (pp. 429–440). Cambridge: Cambridge University Press.

Thorndike, E. L. (1903). *Educational psychology.* New York: Lemke & Buechner.

Thorndike, R. L. (1972). Review of the Torrance Tests of Creative Thinking. In O. K. Buros (Ed.), *The seventh mental measurements yearbook* (pp. 838–839). Highland Park, NJ: Gryphon Press.

Thurstone, L. L. (1938). *Primary mental abilities.* Chicago: University of Chicago Press.

Torrance, E. P. (1966). *The Torrance tests of creative thinking: Norms—technical manual.* Princeton, NJ: Personal Press.

Torrance, E. P. (1972a). Career patterns and peak creative achievements of creative high school students twelve years later. *Gifted Child Quarterly, 16,* 75–88.

Torrance, E. P. (1972b). Predictive validity of the Torrance Tests of Creative Thinking. *Journal of Creative Behavior, 6,* 236–252.

Torrance, E. P. (1974) *The Torrance tests of creative thinking: Norms—technical manual.* Bensenville, IL: Scholastic Testing Service.

Torrance, E. P. (1984). The role of creativity in identification of the gifted and talented. *Gifted Child Quarterly, 28,* 153–156.

Torrance, E. P. (1988). Creativity as manifest in testing. In R. J. Sternberg (Ed.), *The nature of creativity* (pp. 43–75). Cambridge: Cambridge University Press.

Torrance, E. P. (1990). *The Torrance tests of creative thinking: Norms-technical manual.* Bensenville, IL: Scholastic Testing Service.

Torrance, E. P., & Presbury, J. (1984). The criteria of success used in 242 recent experimental studies of creativity. *Creative Child & Adult Quarterly, 9,* 238–243.

Treffinger, D. J. (1986). Research on creativity. *Gifted Child Quarterly, 30,* 15–19.

von Oech, R. (1983). *A whack on the side of the head: How to unlock your mind for innovation.* New York: Warner Books.

Wallace, D. B., & Gruber, H. E. (Eds.). (1989). *Creative people at work: 12 cognitive case studies.* New York: Oxford University Press.

Wallace, P. M., Goldstein, J. H., & Nathan, P. E. (1990). *Introduction to psychology* (2nd ed.). Dubuque, IA: Wm. C. Brown.

Wallach, M. A. (1970). Creativity. In P. H. Mussen (Ed.), *Carmichael's handbook of child psychology* (Vol. 1, 3rd ed., pp. 1211–1272). New York: Wiley.

Wallach, M. A. (1971). *The intelligence/creativity distinction.* Morristown, NJ: General Learning Press.

Wallach, M., & Kogan, N. (1965a). *Modes of thinking in young children.* New York: Holt, Rinehart & Winston.

Wallach, M., & Kogan, N. (1965b). A new look at the creativity–intelligence distinction. *Journal of Personality, 33,* 348–369.

Weisberg, R. W. (1988). Problem solving and creativity. In R. J. Sternberg (Ed.), *The nature of creativity* (pp. 148–176). Cambridge: Cambridge University Press.

Wiggins, G. (1989, November). The futility of trying to teach everything of importance. *Educational Leadership, 47*(3), 44–59.

Williams, F. (1980). *Creativity assessment packet manual.* Buffalo, NY: D. O. K. Publishers.

Willoughby, S., Bereiter, C., Hilton, P., & Rubinstein, J. (1981). *Real Math.* LaSalle, IL: Open Court.

Willoughby, S., Bereiter, C., Hilton, P., Rubinstein, J., Anderson, V., & Scardamalia, M. (1981). *Measuring Bowser.* LaSalle, IL: Open Court.

Willoughby, S., Bereiter, C., Hilton, P., Rubinstein, J., & Scardamalia, M. (1981). *Bargains Galore.* LaSalle, IL: Open Court.

Winner, E. (1982). *Invented worlds: The psychology of the arts.* Cambridge, MA: Harvard University Press.

Yamamoto, K., & Frengel, B. A. (1966). An exploratory component analysis of the Minnesota tests of creative thinking. *California Journal of Educational Research, 17,* 220–229.

# Author Index

# Subject Index

| DATE DUE | | | |
|---|---|---|---|
| JUN 2 5 1998 | | | |
| SEP 3 0 2000 | | | |
| MAY 0 6 | | | |
| | | | |
| | | | |
| | | | |
| | | | |
| | | | |
| | | | |
| | | | |
| | | | |